EXTRE FRUGALITY

SAVE MONEY LIKE YOUR GRANDMA

How to live a creative, happy and sustainable life on much less

By Jane Berry

aka 'Shoestring Jane'

Copyright © Jane Berry, 2022

This book is sold subject to the condition that it shall not, by way of trade or otherwise, be lent, resold, hired out, or otherwise circulated without the publisher's prior consent in any form of binding or cover other than that in which it is published and without a similar condition including this condition being imposed on the subsequent publisher.

No portion of this book may be copied, retransmitted, reposted, duplicated or otherwise used without the express written approval of the author.

Although the author and publisher have made every effort to ensure that the information in this book was correct at the time of being published, the author and publisher do not assume and hereby disclaim any liability to any party for any loss or damage caused by errors or omissions.

The moral right of Jane Berry has been asserted.

Contents

Chapter 1: Frugal Foundations 11
Chapter 2: Stuff, Stuff and More Stuff 19
Chapter 3: Cooking and Eating Like Grandma . 51
Chapter 4: Granny's advice - 'Make do & Mend' and 'Waste Not, Want Not' 91
Chapter 5: Buying Second-Hand and Getting Everything for Less 107
Chapter 6: Slashing Your Monthly Bills 125
Chapter 7: Making a Frugal Home 139
Chapter 8: The Frugal Cleaner 155
Chapter 9: The Frugal Garden 175
Chapter 10: Frugal Fashion: Dress for Less ... 191
Chapter 11: Frugal Fun and Travel 203
Chapter 12: A Frugal Christmas 233
Chapter 13: Health and Well-being on a Budget 251
Chapter 14: It *Is* Easy Being Green 267
References 277
Acknowledgements 287

Introduction

"There is no dignity quite so impressive, and no independence quite so important, as living within your means." – Calvin Coolidge

Some of the best frugal living tips have been handed down from generation to generation. Our war time ancestors had no choice but to make do and mend, to use every bit of food available and, when necessary, to do without. At a time when the global economy has taken a severe hit, we could learn some of the lessons that history has to teach us.

Personally, I love a bit of old-fashioned frugality because it saves me loads of money to spend on things that make me happy! Like days out, experiences and holidays, for example. It means that we can pay our bills on time and live free from the crushing burden of debt.

Frugality – consuming less, wasting less and making the best of what we have – has the added benefit of being good for the environment. In a world that is finally – if belatedly – starting to realise that our planet cannot sustain the rampant consumerism that we have embraced in the past 50 years or so, being more frugal will give you a warm, green glow as well as helping your bank balance.

For the past ten years I have been documenting our lives and sharing tips on frugal living on my blog, Shoestring Cottage and more recently on YouTube. I have discovered a whole community of like-minded people, many living happy and fulfilled lives on very small incomes.

In times of economic austerity and rising inflation, cultivating thrifty habits, using what you have, buying only what you need and eliminating waste from your home can help to cushion you against hard times.

Learning the hard way

As a frugal blogger – aka Shoestring Jane - I am known for my thrifty habits. I buy second-hand, food waste makes me rage and, although I dislike shopping, I will happily spend hours tracking down a bargain when we need something new.

But I wasn't always like that. As with many people, my financial education growing up was non-existent. I thought nothing of going into an unplanned overdraft, of buying my clothes from a catalogue on a weekly repayment plan (at exorbitant expense) or of sticking purchases on my credit card then forgetting to pay it back.

I never had any savings and almost always had some form of debt. In fact, I totally bought into the 'buy now, pay later' culture. Fortunately for me, I never got into serious trouble; I always had a job and could eventually catch up with myself. But my salary rarely lasted the whole month; I was living from pay-cheque to pay-cheque and it wasn't fun.

Divorce in my mid 40's, after 20 years of marriage and three children, was the shock I needed to get my head around my finances.

Suddenly, I was solely responsible for keeping a roof over our heads, for all of our bills and for keeping my daughters fed and clothed. The child maintenance wasn't enough to live on, let alone comfortably. I knew I had to get a grip.

I took a full-time job and made a budget. I began to read all the books I could find on saving money. The internet, I discovered, was also an excellent place to find a wealth of knowledge on all things frugal.

There were many financial failures along the way, as well as sleepless nights worrying about money. Things don't change overnight. For example, as I headed towards my first Christmas as a single parent, I didn't put any funds away for the festivities, so food and presents went on my credit card. This error was swiftly followed by a holiday to Majorca because I wanted to treat my three daughters.

Having spent the following year despairing as a big lump of cash went to pay all this off each month, I vowed not to make the same mistakes again.

Mr Shoestring

Fortunately for me, after my marriage ended I met Justin, known to my blog readers as Mr Shoestring, my partner in frugality. Between us, we have made a lovely home on a budget, complete with a vegetable patch, a climbing rose over the door and a white picket fence.

Before you think we have purchased a Cotswolds cottage, the house we bought was a modest but solid three-bedroom ex-local authority semi. It's really important that your accommodation fits your budget!

In this book, in the spirit of my grandparents' generation, I would like to offer you what I have learned on my frugal journey so far. Depending on your mindset and financial situation, you may find some of it incredibly useful to help cut your bills and curb your spending. It is possible you will dismiss some of my ideas as too extreme or troublesome. But if this book enables you to embrace just some of the spirit of the generation that lived through the second world war then I have achieved my objective.

Good luck on your journey to frugality and financial stability. Get ready to be frugal like your grandma!

A note about resources

Rather than stuff the pages of this book with web addresses, you will find most of them, along with more information about organisations and books mentioned, in the References section at the back.

Chapter 1: Frugal Foundations

"Although no one can go back and make a brand-new start, anyone can start from now and make a brand-new ending." - *Carl Bard*

WHERE TO BEGIN

If you aren't used to the concept of frugal living, it can be hard to know where to begin. In truth, when you are struggling financially, it doesn't really matter where you start as long as you take the first few steps of the journey.

If you are in debt it makes sense to face your financial situation head on, painful as this might be. If you owe money, it is vitally important that you know exactly how much debt you have and work out a plan to pay it off.

I am not a personal finance expert, so won't attempt to offer advice on dealing with debt. However, there is plenty of help out there, so don't stick your head in the sand.

The following organisations in the UK offer free and impartial advice:

Citizens Advice Bureau

Step Change

Pay Plan

National Debtline

Debt Advice Foundation

With good guidance, it is possible to move on from debt. And if you follow the advice on frugality within this book, you can pay off your creditors more quickly and create new and better financial habits for your future.

Making a budget

One of the first steps I took when I decided to take control of my finances was to make a budget. I can hear you sighing with boredom, but stick with me!

I found the idea of scrutinising my money situation so dull (and a bit scary, to be honest), but I forced myself to do it. As I began to feel like I was in charge of my finances, believe me, budgeting became much more interesting.

It can feel like a time-consuming effort to start with, but it soon becomes second nature. These days, I am confident that I know what is coming in and going out and when. Taking my head out of the sand was ultimately very liberating.

To begin with I kept it very simple, with a handwritten table showing my income and outgoings. I wrote down all of my fixed expenses, such as utilities, mortgage, insurances, etc, and set a budget for variable costs like fuel and food.

For the latter, I looked through three months' bank statements and worked out my average grocery spend so that I could set a realistic budget to stick to.

I also put aside an amount on top of the regular bills for car maintenance, clothing, school meals and trips, fun and a small amount for miscellaneous expenses.

As I got better at budgeting, I began to plan ahead and include regular savings for Christmas, birthdays and holidays.

These days I use a budget book, which lives on the dining room table so that I can update and record my spending as I go. However, you might prefer a spreadsheet or an app on your phone. It really doesn't matter. The important thing is to start. Write a budget and become super aware of your spending.

I didn't initially put money aside for an emergency fund, which meant that when (it is usually *when* and not *if*) an appliance broke down or there was an unforeseen expense, I had to dip into the Christmas money.

Eventually I began to follow Dave Ramsey's advice to rectify this. Now I always pay myself first. Money goes into our various saving pots as soon as it arrives and we live on the remainder.

In addition, we aim to have four to six months of living expenses in our contingency account. As Ramsey says, "It is going to rain. You need a rainy-day fund."

There are many ways to budget. It doesn't matter which you choose as long as you find one that works for you. There are various apps and online budgeting tools that can automate the process if you prefer a more high-tech approach.

Review your spending

Part of the process of budgeting and taking control of your finances is to learn where your money is going.

I had only a vague idea of my monthly outgoings when I began this process. All I knew was that there was never any spare at the end of the month and I always hit my overdraft in between pay days.

Writing out my budget made me question some of my spending. I began to ask myself whether certain items were essential, such as my gym membership and a monthly magazine subscription.

I found I was paying insurance on a fridge-freezer that had cost me almost as much as the original purchase price!

Cutting your spending is easier than you think, and we will revisit this many times throughout this book to show you where you might dramatically cut your costs and save money.

Keeping a spending diary

When I took my first steps towards frugality, a spending diary in the form of a small notebook stashed in my handbag allowed me to keep on top of what I had spent on my miscellaneous expenses.

When you can't work out where your money is going, a spending diary can be most revealing. The small purchases really do add up.

Tracking your spending is a bit like tracking your calorie intake. You are sure you don't eat that much, but your waistline tells you otherwise. Once you confront exactly how many biscuits you are consuming and admit to a packet of crisps every evening watching the TV, you soon discover where the extra calories are coming from.

Just like losing weight, spending less can be a challenge. It is too easy to pay out £4 for a take out sandwich, another £5 on a magazine and

£1 on a can of drink. You barely notice the money leaving your wallet but, before you know it, you are a tenner lighter. If you do that every day, that's £70 a week you could be putting into savings or towards your debt.

In my spending diary, I religiously recorded every item I purchased, from the takeout coffee, the amount spent in the supermarket, the cost of a cut and blow dry - everything.

I paid special attention to the small purchases, like newspapers, magazines and chocolate bars. I was surprised at how quickly these added up, especially with three kids in tow!

Keeping such a close eye meant that I knew when I was heading towards the amount I had allowed for these costs. It also meant I could say no to my daughters when they asked for sweets, toys, etc and explain that we had spent our monthly allowance.

Laying these foundations and becoming really familiar with your finances will help you as you begin to move into a more frugal mindset and lifestyle.

Chapter 2: Stuff, Stuff and More Stuff

"Keeping up with the Joneses was a full-time job with my mother and father. It was not until many years later when I lived alone that I realised how much cheaper it was to drag the Joneses down to my level." Quentin Crisp

I'm not interested in filling our house full of things just for the sake of it. Although I don't claim to be a minimalist, stuff for the sake of stuff seems pointless to me and clutter stresses me out.

As the saying goes, the best things in life are not things. So why does modern society spend so much time and money on them?

It's easy nowadays to accumulate stuff and gadgets. It seems as if we are constantly bombarded with the message to 'buy, buy, buy'. We are told that we need the latest phone, the best smart TV, up to the minute fast fashion and a newer, better car. Society encourages us to think nothing of discarding the old and buying new when something loses its sheen. It doesn't matter that the item we are throwing away may be perfectly good and usable; we are always in a rush to get to the next shiny new thing and keep up with everyone else.

We don't try to keep up with the Joneses here at Shoestring Cottage. After all, as Dave Ramsey often says, the Joneses are probably stony broke!

However, it wasn't always like this. I used to feel mad with envy when I saw my friends and family going on expensive holidays, buying beautiful designer clothes and redecorating their entire homes on a whim.

I worked full time yet felt that I had little to show for it. My inner spoiled child shouted that it was unfair! However, when I gave into temptation and made an expensive purchase of furniture or had a holiday, it generally meant long term monthly payments on my credit card and lots of guilt. It wasn't worth it.

I later discovered that many people with superficially perfect lives are often not very content and are frequently nearly suffocating under mountains of debt.

I also found that I could create the home I wanted, dress nicely, eat delicious and healthy food and, yes, take lovely holidays without breaking the bank. By buying second-hand, learning DIY skills, looking for bargains and saving up in advance, we could have a happy and fulfilled life without any spending hangovers.

I learned to live within my means. Who wants to be like the Joneses if they are always arguing about money, or live in a house of cards that may come crashing down around their ears with an unexpected job loss or illness?

Changing my mindset about what truly makes me happy was the crux. If I was stranded forever on a desert island, I wouldn't be desperate for a pile of fashionable clothes, a designer kitchen or the latest car.

As long as I had something to eat and somewhere safe to sleep, it would be my family and friends, my pets, a beautiful view, a walk with Mr Shoestring, hours spent pottering in the garden, music, some decent books or a great film or two that I would crave. Recognising the pleasures that can be found in simple things may be a cliché, but it's also a reality for me.

I come across lots of folk who happily live in a sea of debt because they know they can make the monthly repayments. But what happens if something changes?

Our 2020 Covid-19 experience has taught the world that no one's job is 100% safe and no one is immune to illness or misfortune. This is why you should have an emergency fund. Practising some old-fashioned frugality will help you save for one!

DO IT FOR THE PLANET

As someone who has been banging on about this stuff for many years, I am heartened to see that there is finally an awareness growing about the need to change our consumerist lifestyle.

Our great grandparents would have been amazed at our wasteful lifestyles. They wouldn't have known what a single use item was – everything was used again and again because they had much less and placed more value on what they owned. They didn't waste stuff, because they couldn't afford to.

If we could mentally step back into their shoes we could go a long way to resolving our current climate crisis and the mess we have made of the environment.

Old fashioned frugality would mean we would baulk at single use plastics and never dream of wasting food. We would wear our clothes until they either didn't fit or fell apart, at which point they would be passed on or turned into something else. Fuel wouldn't be squandered – we would make our transport and our homes as energy efficient as possible to keep our bills low.

STOP SHOPPING FOR STUFF YOU DON'T NEED

Canadian illustrator Sarah Lazarovic plays on Maslow's Hierarchy of Needs pyramid to create a Buyerarchy of Needs instead. Following this idea could help you become a self-actualised, waste nothing, anti-consumer!

At the bottom of the pyramid, the largest section, she urges you to use what you have. The next level suggests borrowing rather than buying. Layer four is swapping, layer three is thrifting, layer two is making and the very top of the pyramid, layer 1, is buying.

It might be helpful to consider the Buyerarchy of Needs next time you feel like making a spontaneous purchase.

HOW TO BREAK THE SHOPPING HABIT

If you have a serious shopping habit, how do you stop yourself from buying things you don't need? Are you an emotional shopper? Or do you shop because you are bored? I have been guilty of both in the past. It can be so hard to find the willpower to stop spending sometimes.

These days it is just too easy to spend money. We don't even need to leave the comfort of our armchairs to have a splurge. You can be idly browsing the internet one minute and have a virtual shopping basket full of goods the next.

I am no shopaholic, but if I am not careful, I can easily pop into town for one thing and come back with another four items that I didn't realise I *needed* until I saw them.

If you want to pay off debt or build your savings, how can you learn to resist temptation and stop spending? Here are some techniques that I have found helpful.

1 Avoid temptation

This is my number one way to stop spending. If I don't hit the shops or look online then I rarely spend anything. I know that I don't need a lot of stuff and I don't shop as a leisure activity.

This includes charity shops, which are a weakness for me. Even if they are full of amazing bargains, if I don't need any of them I am wasting my money and bringing clutter home.

If you have retailer apps on your phone, you could begin by deleting them. You can even use parental restrictions to block the sites you are most tempted by! Anything that makes it harder to impulse shop may be helpful. (An internet search will tell you how to block certain websites on any device.)

2 Stop spending on the small stuff

Even if you resist actually going shopping, it is easy to forget that small purchases really do add up. A coffee on the way to work, a magazine at lunch time, or a couple of glasses of wine with colleagues at the end of the day are the culprits that once busted my budget.

If you find money being leached from your bank account because of a lot of inexpensive items, try my trick and begin to keep a spending diary.

Seeing in black and white how much money you waste on avoidable purchases can help get you back on track.

3 Don't shop with children

If you have kids around it is even harder to keep on top of unnecessary spending. Not only do you have to resist your own inner shopping demons, you need to stand firm against your children's constant pleas.

If it is remotely possible to leave them at home, even if you are just grocery shopping, then do. Even now that my three daughters are adults, I still spend more if they are with me.

4 Set a budget and track your spending

As I mentioned previously, setting a budget – and keeping track of it - was the action that finally gave me control of my spending. I know how much I have at the beginning of the month, how much my bills are going to be and the amount that will go into savings. What is left over has to last the month.

5 Set clear goals

Having a goal to aim for can really focus your attention and help you to stop spending.

Try to make your goals specific. Rather than saying 'I want to pay off my debts', say 'I will pay off £100 towards my credit card every month'.

One of my goals is always to put a fixed amount each month into my emergency savings fund and the same figure into a holiday/birthday fund.

Make your goal measurable and achievable. You will feel positive and inspired when you manage to achieve it.

6 Avoid the sales

The sales are a dangerous time! It is so easy to tell yourself it is okay to make a purchase when an item is 50% off. This is one of the reasons I often have a no-spend January, when the sales hit a peak. By the time I dust off my wallet in February the danger has usually passed.

However, if there is something very specific that you need, saving up and then waiting until you know there will be a discount is obviously a good strategy.

7 Hide your credit cards or cut them up

I have a single credit card for emergency use only. I don't take it out with me unless I am going on holiday. It is hidden away in a drawer so that I am not tempted to grab it at home to make an online impulse purchase.

I have heard people suggest freezing your credit card in a container full of water – I think this is genius!

Dave Ramsey would advise you not to have a credit card at all (his motto is, 'cash is king'). I think that this is a good idea if you are a serious shopaholic. Cut it into a million pieces and throw it away. Which leads onto…

8 Use cash

Cash is harder to spend than credit or debit cards. You can feel the money in your hand and you can see it leaving you. It hurts more to hand over the paper stuff than flash your debit card over the pay machine.

Also, it stands to reason that if you go out to make a purchase with £20 in cash and no debit or credit cards, then £20 is all you are going to spend.

9 Have regular no-spend periods

Challenge yourself to regular no-spend days, weeks or even months. Once I have set a rule that I am buying nothing except essentials for a set period, I find it easy to stop spending. The rule is absolute, so there is no arguing with myself or anyone else. No, I can't go out to dinner/the pub/the cinema, I am on a no spend month. Yes, new shoes would be nice, but actually I am on a no spend week so I will wear one of the 10 pairs already in the cupboard.

10 Unsubscribe from newsletters

I try not to get sucked in to subscribing to updates or newsletters when I make an online purchase. However, sometimes those clever companies make it easy to miss the little box you have to tick. Just unsubscribe when they come through, then you won't be constantly tempted by special offers and discounts.

11 Cancel catalogues

If you still receive glossy catalogues through the post, cancel those too. Put any you have lying around in the recycling. They make everything look so beautiful and tempting!

12 Don't buy glossy magazines

These are even worse than catalogues. They present the perfect (expensive) lifestyle that can make you feel dissatisfied and envious.

It's easy to feel rubbish if your home doesn't look as stunning as those in the carefully set up scenes, your garden isn't full of expensive furniture or exotic plants or you haven't got a wardrobe full of immaculate clothes like the stick thin models.

Who do you know that actually lives like that? In reality, most of us cope with furniture scratched by the cats or damaged by children and time. Rather than wearing designer outfits and a full face of makeup, we wander round in our trackie bottoms and no bra as often as we can get away with it!

13 Get organised

If you want to keep your spending to a minimum, get organised. Keep a running shopping list and plan your meals. You are much less likely to buy food you won't use or give in to a take away if you know what is for dinner each night.

When you are out and about, take refreshments. I don't even go into town without a water bottle and often even a flask of coffee. I keep a stash of cereal bars in my bag as well. Occasionally I love a coffee or cup of tea in a cafe, but this can become an expensive habit if you aren't careful.

14 Don't fall into the 'I deserve it' trap

I remember when I first had a Saturday job in a shop, aged 16. One of my colleagues often said (as she spent most of her pay packet before she had even left the shop), 'A working gal needs to treat herself'. For a while I followed her example, but pretty soon realised I was just handing my employer back my hard-earned wages!

It's really easy to fall into the trap of treating yourself because you have been working hard, or feeling poorly, or are a bit down... Just remember what your goals are and how much better you will feel when you make it to the end of the month with no overdraft.

15 Shop from your cupboards

When I feel tempted to buy new clothes because I 'have nothing to wear', I go through everything I already own. A wardrobe declutter will always reveal some gems I have forgotten about.

Do the same with your books, CDs (if you are old fashioned, like me!), kitchen gadgets, tools, etc. This will take your mind off the temptation to buy something new and you might even find some unwanted items worth selling. Which brings me to…

16 Sell instead of buy

As another distraction technique for the shopaholic, how about going through the stuff you already have and making some money? There aren't many folks in the Western world who don't have lots of extraneous possessions - items that were purchased on impulse and not used, things you no longer use or bits and pieces that you bought for a particular occasion but only needed once.

I am a big fan of decluttering as a kind of therapy. It makes me feel in control, and living a (slightly) more minimalist lifestyle is less stressful.

If you can sell some of the things you declutter and put the money towards your savings goals or paying debt, you get a double benefit. Time for a spring clean, maybe?

17 Avoid saying 'I've blown the budget already so…'

Once you have given into temptation, it suddenly becomes so much easier to spend more money. This is odd, as you might think the opposite would be the case.

I find once I have loosened the purse strings a bit I need to be careful not to go crazy with my spending. It is easy to think, 'Oh well, I have blown the budget now, I might as well get this too'. Be aware if this is something that you are prone to and try to extract yourself from temptation as quickly as possible.

18 Build in treats

If you need to stick to a tight budget, it is important to build in some treats. A sense of deprivation and resentment can soon set in if you don't, no matter how determined you are. A weekly takeaway, an occasional trip to the cinema or whatever you fancy will be guilt free and more enjoyable when you know you can afford it.

19 Beg, borrow, share

This takes us back to the Buyerarchy of Needs. As many of your family and friends will have useful items such as steam cleaners, hedge trimmers and various power tools that don't get used frequently, ask to borrow rather than choosing to buy new. You can offer the use of whatever gizmo you already own in exchange.

Join an organisation such as Freecycle or Freegle and see what is being given away for free. You can also post wanted ads for particular items. Just don't be one of those annoying people who always takes without occasionally giving, though.

20 Understand your triggers

Often your triggers for spending are obvious when you start to think about them. PMT, a tough day at work, loneliness, boredom… Try to identify yours so that you can develop a strategy to deal with them without spending money.

If you are bored or lonely, how about volunteering? If your spending patterns are filling some kind of void in your life, maybe it is possible to find another way to feel happy.

21 The money saver's chant

Can I afford this? Do I really need it? Do I really want it? Will I still need it tomorrow?

Learn the money saver's chant! The more you ask yourself these questions before each purchase, the more likely they are to become a habit.

WHAT CAN YOU STOP BUYING?

There are many items that we view as essentials today that our great grandparents wouldn't have recognised at all, let alone seen as necessities. They would have been bemused by many of them!

Below is a list of some of the things I no longer buy, both to save money and reduce the waste we produce. Of course, you may genuinely feel that you can't do without some of the items on my list, but hopefully my suggestions will provide food for thought.

Some of these objects create a lot of waste and pollution. From the chemicals they are made from, the plastics that package them, and the energy used to produce and transport them, if at least some of them didn't exist the planet would be all the better for it.

There are often reusable alternatives for these items, and these are becoming easier to find. They may cost more initially, but can save quite a lot of money over time.

These inessential items also add to your shopping bill. If you are on a tight budget, you might find that you can do without them altogether. Certainly, reducing the number of things you buy on a regular basis will help you to build up that cushion against emergencies or save for something you really need or want.

Another advantage of not buying unnecessary stuff is that you end up with less clutter in your home.

20 THINGS I DON'T BUY TO SAVE MONEY AND WASTE

1 Air fresheners

I really dislike air fresheners. Not only do they not 'freshen' the air, they fill it with chemical pollutants that you and your family then inhale.

A can of spray air freshener somehow made it into our house about five years ago. Since none of us bother with it, it is sitting redundant on the loo. I won't throw it out until it is empty, as maybe visitors will use it.

The plug-in air fresheners that spurt out perfume every so often are the worst. They actually make me feel unwell.

2 Liquid soap

I stopped buying liquid soap years ago. The solid stuff is nicer I think, and comes in just a fraction of the packaging. It is also much cheaper than liquid soap. I try to buy it wrapped in card or paper rather than plastic film if I can.

3 Services I can do myself

These vary from time to time with me, but generally speaking I do my own house cleaning, wash my own car, dye my hair, decorate the house and tend the garden. In fact, I thoroughly enjoy the latter - free exercise!

I have even been known to cut my own hair, but I don't have the skills to do it all the time. The fringe is easy enough and I can take the ends off, but wouldn't like to take more than a few centimetres off. Some things are best left to the professionals.

However, I do appreciate that some folk work longer hours than I do, may have a disability that prevents them doing a lot of physical activity or don't have a handy Mr Shoestring to help, so these may not be possible for everyone.

4 Bottled water

These days I am pretty good at remembering to take a reusable water bottle with me. On the rare occasions I forget, if I have to buy a bottle of water it then gets reused several times.

We are fortunate to have safe, clean tap water in the UK, so why people buy the bottled stuff to drink at home is a mystery to me. It creates a huge amount of plastic waste as well as adding to the grocery bill.

If you find your tap water smells and tastes of chlorine, try pouring a jug full and leaving it on the side or in your fridge for a couple of hours. You will find the taste and smell quickly dissipate.

5 Useless gifts

I would rather give someone money or a voucher to be spent on an item they really want than purchase a generic gift set or novelty present that will end up in the charity bag or - worst of all - the bin.

In my view, it is always best to ask what a family member or friend would like for birthdays and Christmas. A surprise is only a good idea if you know the person really well!

If your budget is really small, a home-made cake or other consumable item can be a good idea. For example, if you keep house plants, you can take cuttings and pot them up as cheap and eco-friendly gifts.

6 Loads of different cleaning products

Advertisers are very good at making us believe we need a different, chemical laden product for each area of our homes. What's the difference between a cleaning spray for the kitchen and one for the bathroom? Very little, I would suggest.

All of these things come in plastic bottles with unrecyclable nozzles. I prefer to use more natural items like bicarbonate of soda and vinegar, which can be used throughout the house. See Chapter 8 for more information on frugal cleaning products that also happen to be healthier and more eco-friendly.

I no longer have a cupboard bursting at the seams with miscellaneous products, so there is less clutter as well.

7 Coffee pods and filters

Much as I enjoy a good cup of coffee, I am no connoisseur. A decent instant is good enough for me, although I do love to bubble up the milk with my little coffee frother, which was a birthday gift from my daughters. It makes my home-made coffee look and taste just like one from Starbucks.

I don't like all the waste that comes with pods and filters, plus they are more expensive.

8 Cotton wool pads

I used to get through masses of cotton wool pads to take my makeup off. Now I prefer to use washable and reusable bamboo ones.

They work just as well, and come with a little drawstring bag which can be tossed straight into the washing machine.

9 Disposable razors

I haven't bought a disposable plastic razor since Christmas 2018, when my daughter purchased me a reusable safety razor made from bamboo and stainless steel.

The blades last for ages if you rinse and dry them after each use, and the razor itself should pretty much last forever.

10 Pre-chopped meat and vegetables

I have never understood why people are prepared to pay so much more to have their carrots sliced or their chicken breast chopped up. Unless you have a mobility issue that makes food prep tricky, of course, in which case ready chopped food is likely worth the cost.

In the case of vegetables in particular, you end up with a lot more plastic packaging when you buy pre-chopped. As it literally takes a few seconds to chop my own, I buy whole vegetables, meat and salad items.

I make an exception for yellow stickered (reduced) items, which save money and stop the food going to waste.

11 New clothing

OK, I can't hand on heart say I NEVER buy new clothing. I always purchase my underwear from new and I do buy a new dress once in a while.

However, generally speaking, there is very little in my wardrobe that wasn't purchased second-hand. I am not a fan of fast fashion because it is so wasteful and polluting. Also, by buying pre-owned clothes, I can afford better quality.

12 Disposable dishcloths

I can't remember the last time I bought a disposable dishcloth. The cloth ones are better in my opinion, as long as they are washed frequently. I also soak them in a little disinfectant or bleach most evenings so that they don't collect bacteria.

When they are too tatty for the dishes they go in the cleaning basket to do the bathroom.

13 Shower gel

I have never got on with shower gel. Too faffy when you have water in your eyes! As with hand soap, I find shower gel is a pointless expense and another way to avoid plastic bottles.

14 Christmas cards

I haven't bought any Christmas cards for a few years now, partly because I accumulated such a large stash I haven't needed to! Christmas cards are things you can easily pick up each year, forgetting you have a box from the previous festive period.

However, a few Christmases ago I decided not to send any at all, partly to save money and partly to prevent waste. The vast majority of cards will end up being thrown away come the new year anyway.

And guess what? The world didn't end and I am pretty sure no one even noticed. I sent personal messages to family and friends via email, although my non-digital elderly relatives did get one of the stash sent to them.

15 Christmas wrap

I no longer buy any Christmas wrap either. Instead, I use the collection of gift bags that I always keep when receiving presents. I also have some wrap from gifts that I carefully remove and fold for reuse.

I look out for scraps of fabric and old scarves when I am at the charity shop as these make lovely, reusable gift wrappings. The recipients of my gifts mostly give them back as soon as the gifts have been opened but some keep them to use again themselves.

16 Newspapers and magazines

I get my news online, from the TV or from the radio, so I no longer need to buy newspapers.

Fortunately, I kicked my magazine habit years ago. They may be pretty and glossy, but they are also incredibly expensive and full of adverts for things I can't afford or don't want anyway.

17 Clothes that are dry clean only

The only things I have purchased that are dry clean have been second-hand items of clothing that I think I can risk careful handwashing. Honestly, apart from tailored suits or coats with a high wool content, why does anything need to be dry cleaned?

It's not only coats and jackets either. I have come across dresses and tops that need to be dry cleaned. As most people would only wear these once or twice at the most, that is one expensive piece of clothing! The dry-cleaning process also involves a lot of nasty chemicals, so no thanks.

18 Disposable plates, cups and cutlery

I used to buy these for parties, especially when my kids were small. Then I worked out it was better to invest in some plastic beakers to bring out on these occasions, for the children anyway.

Now I always use real plates, cutlery and glasses. I have enough for my extended family, mainly bought second-hand at boot sales and in charity shops. There is also a stash of cheap glass wine goblets under the bed.

19 Premium branded groceries

I have never believed that branded groceries are that much superior to supermarket own brands, so I avoid them (with one or two exceptions. There is a brand of coffee that I love, but look out for it on special offer and stock up).

I don't go for the premium 'finest' supermarket items either. They tend to be for pre-prepared and processed dishes that I can make myself.

20 Canned soup

I absolutely love making - and eating - soup! It is the frugal cook's friend, as you can make it from pretty much anything and use up all your odds and ends.

All good soup starts with a decent stock - you can make your own from your poultry carcasses or vegetable peelings.

Once you have got into making soup, you will never want to eat the canned stuff again. I find it too sweet or salty as well as being full of cheap ingredients to thicken it.

You don't need a special soup maker either, just a large pan, a knife and maybe a hand blender if you like a smooth consistency.

Once you get started, no doubt you will find many more things to trim from your life and your budget and save yourself from what James Wallman calls 'stuffocation'.

If you need more inspiration to rid your life of pointless clutter, his book *Stuffocation: Living More With Less* is a worthwhile read.

Chapter 3: Cooking and Eating Like Grandma

"I'm frugal. I'm not a very acquisitive woman. I never waste food. If you prepare your own food, you engage with the world, it tastes alive. It tastes good." - Vivienne Westwood

Cooking skills are no longer taught well in our schools. Many families live off takeaways and convenience foods. However, your kitchen is the first place to go if you want to go back to some old-fashioned frugality.

Learning to cook from scratch is an essential life skill. Knowing that you can confidently throw the ingredients you have to hand together to make a basic meal will save a lot of money.

I am not talking about Cordon Bleu food here. Just knowing how to make a pasta sauce, a casserole, a pie or even bangers and mash will mean you can cut some of your 'ping' meals off the shopping list. You are also less likely to give in to the lure of the take-away dinner if you begin to enjoy making delicious meals yourself for far less.

I am old enough to have learned quite a lot about cooking in my domestic science classes in school. I regret that this is barely offered at all now. It is a mistake in my view. Nurturing young people who can cook and understand nutrition would go a long way to improving the nation's health.

In my teens I became vegetarian for a time. This forced me to learn much more about food, since my parents didn't want to have to make me something separate for each meal. It did me a favour and enabled me to hone my culinary skills for life.

LEARNING TO COOK WILL SAVE YOU MONEY

Having to fend for myself as a newbie vegetarian was a good experience for me as I found I really loved throwing things together and being a little creative with food. Even though I eat meat these days, I still have this somewhat haphazard and adventurous approach to cooking, which is handy when I have to combine various ingredients that need eating into something edible. Although, I have to admit, this does very occasionally turn out to be an experiment I do not want to repeat!

I cannot claim to create anything of restaurant quality in the kitchen, but I can reliably pull together a nice meal for very little money.

I am very proud that my three daughters can all cook too, as I had them chopping veg, making simple meals and baking from a very early age. I swear that this led to them being very easy to feed and not at all fussy. If I had happened to have sons, I would have done the same!

I used to tear my hair out when their friends came for tea and wouldn't touch a vegetable or anything that didn't come out of a box in the freezer. They usually went home hungry.

As well as teaching your children a skill that will help them stay physically and financially healthy for life, involving your kids with the process of creating dinner will make them much more likely to eat and enjoy it.

FOOD WASTE AND HOW TO PREVENT IT

During World War II, no one wasted any food. In fact, it was illegal in Britain. Anything that couldn't be eaten for any reason went into the collection bins to feed the pigs.

Even today, can you imagine people in the developing world chucking away a lettuce because it has passed its best before date, or fruit because it looks a little wrinkled? It wouldn't happen!

According to the Waste and Resources Action Programme (WRAP), in the UK we waste 6.6 million tonnes of food a year, most of which is perfectly usable. This is like throwing money in the bin. On top of that, the greenhouse gases that arise from this wasted food are a contributing factor in our changing climate.

In western countries particularly, we have so much choice and quantity, we no longer value the time, effort and expense of growing, packaging, transporting and retailing food. We take our never-ending supplies for granted.

One way to avoid food waste is to learn to use leftovers. Occasionally, despite planning our meals, we simply cook too much. Personally, I love it when I don't have to make lunch because there is some of the previous evening's meal in the fridge for me!

However, sometimes we forget about stuff at the back of the fridge, or are too tired or uninspired to use ingredients before they go a bit manky. Occasionally, most of us collect non-perishables that are perfectly usable, but have been sitting in the cupboard for months or even years.

This is where a bit of creativity comes in handy. However you do it, aim to use these forgotten items. Plan them into your weekly meal plan. Have the odd week where you try to eat exclusively from your stores of food rather than buying more.

If you live alone or in a smaller household, it can be a better idea to buy frozen rather than fresh where feasible. This way you can take out and cook only what you will eat in one sitting, with nothing wasted.

STORING FOOD CORRECTLY

It is important that you store food correctly to prevent waste, and in some cases, food poisoning. There are a few basic rules to follow.

1 Keep your fridge cool

Make sure your fridge is cold enough. It should be set at between 0 and 5°C.

Try to minimise how often it is opened and shut it as quickly as possible. Don't put hot food straight into the fridge or freezer; allow it to cool first.

2 Read the label

It sounds obvious, but make sure you check food labels and follow storage instructions. For example, some condiments such as Worcestershire sauce don't require refrigeration after opening, but others, like mayonnaise, do.

3 Storing meat

Raw meat should be stored in the fridge in a sealed container on the bottom shelf, so that it can't drip onto other items.

You shouldn't use meat after its use by date. However, use your common sense with this. Sometimes you can tell by the smell, look and feel of meat whether it is still safe to eat, even if the label says it is within date.

Freeze meat if you can't eat it before its expiry date. I often find very good reductions in the supermarket on meat close to or on the use by date. This saves money, so do look out for those yellow sticker items and freeze them immediately if you can't use them the same day.

Don't mix cooked and raw meats - store and prepare them separately.

If you won't use leftover meat within two days, freeze it in a labelled container and use it in an upcoming meal plan fairly quickly so you don't forget about it.

Meat that has previously been frozen and then cooked can be cooled quickly and refrozen. However, do not freeze raw meat (or anything else) more than once.

Meat is best defrosted overnight in a container in your fridge.

4 Vegetables

Store your raw vegetables correctly. Most are best wrapped or kept in their packaging in the bottom of your fridge.

Keep spuds in a cool, dark place and don't buy more than you will use before they begin sprouting or going green.

If you buy items loose, you could put them into plastic storage boxes with lids so they keep their crunch longer. However, mushrooms are best stored in a paper bag to avoid them going slimy.

5 Fresh fruit

Remember that fruits such as bananas and avocados emit ethylene gas, which speeds up the ripening process. Useful if you have under-ripe fruit you want to eat soon, but otherwise store these items away from other fruit.

Soft fruits such as grapes and berries should always be refrigerated and used quickly. Stone fruit such as peaches are best left to ripen in the fruit bowl. However, check them regularly, and place them in the fridge when they are almost ripe.

When the weather is hot I tend to store all fruit apart from bananas in the fridge, to avoid any spoiled, mouldy items. I also refuse to buy bananas more than two or three at a time in the summer - unless I want some overripe ones for a cake!

6 Non-perishable items

Store non-perishable items such as flour, rice and pasta in sealed packaging or containers. Keep them off the floor in an area that doesn't get either too damp or too warm.

When you open a can but don't use all the contents, transfer to a suitable container and cover to store in the fridge. Once open, the contents can react with the tin, so tin cans aren't suitable for storing food.

Flour should be stored in a cool, dark place in an airtight container. It will last longer in the fridge, but you can also freeze it. This preserves it for up to a year. Freezing your flour will kill off any pests and prevent weevil contamination.

BEST BEFORE AND USE BY LABELS

Much has been said and written about the problems of best before and use by dates. When consumers blindly follow best before dates particularly, they end up throwing out perfectly good, usable food.

Best before dates are an indication of the likely quality of the food if it has been hanging around for a while, not whether it is safe to eat.

Take canned food, for example. As long as there is no damage to the container, it will last literally years and years. It may not taste as good if it is 10 years out of date, but it won't kill you if the can isn't damaged. Never eat canned food that has 'blown'; if you push the top of the can and it pops, it indicates that the contents may be infected and could give you botulism.

Use by dates are a different story, although personally I often ignore them for a day or two if something smells and tastes good. I have often cooked fruit that is a little soft and wrinkly, or used it in a smoothie. Veg and salads are safe to eat even if they look a bit limp, although there will be some loss of nutrients.

I am a lot more cautious with meat and fish, but have eaten dairy products, cheese, butter, dips and hummus several days after the best before date, with no ill effects.

However, I am not advocating that you do this! There is a risk of food poisoning such as listeria or salmonella when you eat something beyond its use by date, particularly if it hasn't been stored in a cold enough fridge.

Some bold folk laugh in the face of potential food poisoning and eat things that are way past the expiry date. In the US, a blogger called Scott Nash, who is also the CEO of an organic food chain, decided to spend a year eating out of date food and blogging about it. Nash started with a yoghurt that was six months out of date and suffered no ill effects, so he decided to experiment further, eating out of date pesto, smoked trout, minced beef and more.

It does make you wonder if the food industry is a tad over cautious when setting these dates. You can check out Scott Nash's experiment on his blog, Scott's Compost Pile.

HOW TO USE LEFTOVERS

I am quite good at using up leftovers. As I said before, sometimes they are welcome. They either get eaten for lunch or we have them two days in a row. Alternatively, I anticipate leftovers from one meal and incorporate them into another. For example, too much cooked veg one day can become the basis for a soup or stew the following day.

The usual advice is to use leftovers stored in the fridge within two days. (We have found that properly cooked food usually lasts up to a week, but use your senses and don't risk wasting it.)

If I can't eat it quickly enough, I use my freezer to conserve even the smallest amounts of leftover food. The challenge is then to remember what I have frozen and work it into my meal planning to ensure it is used up. I recommend labelling and dating everything that you freeze.

In the end, smarter planning and shopping will stop you having so many leftovers in the first place. Keeping track of what you have already and storing it correctly will also help.

Nevertheless, none of us is perfect. Even with good planning we occasionally end up with more than we can eat before it spoils. With a bit of determination and creativity, we can all reduce food waste.

USING IT UP

Here are some ideas for using foods that are commonly left over to reduce food waste and save yourself some money.

1 Bread ends

Unless you have a large family and eat lots of bread, it pays to keep a sliced loaf in the freezer and remove slices as you plan to use them. They defrost in around 10 minutes. However, even if you do this, what to do with the bread ends?

The obvious thing is to make bread crumbs – whizz them up in a food processor or grate them by hand. If they come from a fresh loaf I like to freeze them for when they are required.

Bread pudding, apple brown betty, bread and butter pudding, croutons and bread sauce can all be made using the crusts of bread.

2 Potatoes

Leftover mashed potatoes are easy to use up in lots of dishes. Indeed, sometimes I deliberately make too much so that I can add them to soup as a thickener. They can also be made into fish cakes, added to a meat or nut loaf, chucked into soups and stews, or transformed into the classic bubble and squeak, which will use up your uneaten green veggies as well.

Whole cooked potatoes are a treat sliced, fried and served with a couple of eggs and some baked beans for brunch or supper.

3 Cooked vegetables

You can chop up your uneaten cooked vegetables and throw them into an omelette or frittata. Soup is another way to use them: I keep an old plastic pot in the freezer and put all unwanted cooked vegetables in it for my regular soup-making sessions.

Many leftover vegetables are nice in a pasta sauce too, although I probably wouldn't use sprouts or cabbage in this way (I know some people would!).

4 Fresh herbs

Have you ever bought a load of parsley or coriander for a recipe and left the rest of it to go soggy in your fridge? Yes, me too. However, there is nothing lovelier than a cheese and chopped herb omelette for lunch or dinner. You can cut herbs up and put them in a salad too.

If you have a lot of a particular herb you can chop finely and freeze. You can even dry them yourself.

Another way to use herbs is to add them to a bottle of olive oil to give it extra flavour.

5 Gravy

Proper gravy made with the juices from the roast is always a treat. It is certainly too good to chuck in the bin.

Gravy will keep a couple of days in the fridge so you could make a point of using it at another meal. It will also add lots of flavour to a casserole or soup or you can freeze it to use another day.

Leftover gravy adds depth to a shepherd's pie or you could use it as a kind of cook-in sauce with meatballs. How about mixing it with leftover meat or vegetables as a pie filling?

6 Rice and pasta

You have to be careful with rice. Once it is cooked, it needs to be kept cool and eaten quickly. Don't leave it lying around or bacteria can build up that can cause food poisoning.

It is another leftover ingredient that I freeze to add to soup, but it can be fried up with an egg and some veg for a DIY egg fried rice, made into a kind of risotto with lots of vegetables and some tomatoes, used for rice salad or transformed into some delicious cheesy rice balls.

Leftover pasta is also good made into a salad or to thicken soups and stews.

I find it best to measure both before cooking, however, so that we have the correct amount for the dish.

7 Bananas

Banana loaf or muffins are so delicious I almost want the bananas to turn black so that I can bake some! You can also freeze bananas in slices to add to smoothies or you could make them into an easy vegan chocolate ice cream. All you have to do is blend one frozen banana with 1 teaspoon of cocoa powder for a healthy, dairy-free treat.

8 Apples

We seem to have gone off apples in our household. The last few times I have bought them they have turned wrinkly in the fruit bowl. Fortunately, we are all happy to eat them stewed with custard. They also freeze well peeled and sliced or you can dry them in the oven.

To do this, cut them into rings and place flat on a baking sheet. Sprinkle over some cinnamon and place them in the oven on its lowest setting for about six hours. Leave the oven door slightly ajar to allow the condensation to escape. Apples can also be dried in a single layer in an air fryer in around 10 minutes, which is a more energy efficient option.

My favourite way to use up apples is in a crumble or in spiced apple cake.

9 Citrus fruit

If you don't use a whole lemon or lime in one go, freeze it in segments to pop straight into your G&T (or sparkling water if you are better behaved). You could also freeze the juice in ice cube trays for when you need it in a recipe.

Dry citrus peels for baking. Chop them up and spread them onto a baking sheet, then put them in a really low oven – about 80 degrees centigrade for around two hours. Allow them to cool completely before storing them in a glass container.

Citrus peels are great for home-made cleaning products. See Chapter 8 for more information on frugal cleaning.

10 Wilting salad

These days I try to buy small amounts of salad at a time. I make sure it is built into our meal plan so that we use it. However, wilting salad leaves do get thrown into our soups and stir fries and no one is ever the wiser.

Add chopped spring onion tops to mashed potatoes or mix with cheese to fill a jacket spud.

11 Other odds and ends

Doughnuts are best eaten on the day they are purchased, but if you happen to have some left over, pop them in the microwave for 20 seconds to revive them.

Omelettes and quiches are good for using up all kinds of cooked veg, ham, bacon and hard cheeses.

Risottos are also perfect for using your leftovers. You can chuck in cooked meat, pulses, vegetables and herbs.

So many things can be frozen. For example, you can freeze leftover wine for cooking. Hard cheeses can also be stored in the freezer, although it's a good idea to grate them first for ease of use.

HOW TO MAKE STOCK

If, like me, you love to make soup, then making your own stock first is a great way to save your meat bones and vegetable scraps from the bin.

I often keep chicken carcasses in the freezer for this very purpose. It seems a crying shame to throw meat bones out when you can get more nutritional value from them in this way.

For a bone broth, I buy a large bag of bones from the butcher, then use in the same way as the poultry stock method below. However, I tend to cook this long and slow to get maximum flavour.

A slow cooker is great for making stock, if you have one that is large enough. Cook on low for eight hours.

Poultry stock method

You ideally need at least two carcasses to make a good poultry stock. Put your poultry carcasses in a big pot with a couple of carrots, an onion chopped in half, three sticks of celery, two bay leaves and about six black peppercorns. Add enough cold water to cover. Put on the pan lid and bring to the boil, then simmer for around three hours. Strain over another pan or large jug and you will have tasty and nutritious stock.

Vegetable stock method

Home-made vegetable stock is so easy and means that you can use all the trimmings and peelings from your veg that might go in the compost, food waste bin or even in your trash. It is a way to take every last bit of goodness from your food, as many of the vitamins are directly under the skin.

Collect up your veg peelings and trimmings, keeping them in a container in the freezer. Once you have a couple of containers full, it is time to make the stock. Really anything will do, but I don't use the peel from onions as I find them bitter.

All you need to do is place your vegetable peelings in a large saucepan with an onion chopped in half, a stick of celery sliced in two, 10 or so black peppercorns and a couple of bay leaves. Just cover with water and bring to the boil. Add a teaspoon or two of salt. Put on the pan lid and simmer for two hours.

PRESERVING

Of course, the home preservation of fruit and vegetables was commonplace for our grandparents and great-grandparents. In recent years, as growing your own has come back into fashion, many of us have been reviving some of the old ways to preserve the harvest.

If you have a glut of fruit, it is easy and satisfying to make some jam or jelly. There are lots of recipes online. Chutney making and pickling are also fairly straightforward.

In the US, canning food seems to be quite common still, although you need to know what you are doing to avoid the perils of botulism!

You do need some equipment, such as a preserving pan to make jams and pickles, but these can often be found second-hand.

The subject of preserving is a subject of its own, of course. If you would like to try it, it is worth finding a good book on the subject.

OTHER WAYS TO REDUCE YOUR GROCERY BUDGET

Not wasting food is only part of the story. There are many other frugal tricks to reduce your food budget.

1 Eat like a peasant

Every culture has a tradition of 'peasant food': dishes created from cheap, local ingredients in a way that made them not only palatable, but delicious. These peasant dishes are often highly prized today - and are not always that cheap if you happen to come across them in a restaurant!

Nevertheless, you can still take inspiration from the creativity of our practical, cash-strapped ancestors and learn how to make good food with what is available.

Think of cassoulet, the French stew made with beans, vegetables and small amounts of meat, shepherd's pie - stewed mince and vegetables with a topping of filling mashed potatoes to fill you up - or meat loaves, which pop up in many cultures, made from scraps of meat extended with bread, grains and vegetables.

Peasant food was based on what was growing at certain times of the year. Even today, buying food seasonally, when it is fresh and plentiful, can provide a cheaper basis for your meals. If you are blessed with a good local market, this will be the most economical place to buy food in season, but there are some deals to be had at the supermarkets as well.

2 Stretch your ingredients

You can make a new tradition of peasant food and stretch more expensive ingredients like meat or fish with cheaper vegetables, grains and pulses.

Try adding a cup of cooked lentils, oatmeal or a can of baked beans to the mince when you are making a cottage pie, chilli or Bolognese sauce. Hearty amounts of onions, potatoes and root veg with smaller amounts of meat will make a delicious one pot dinner in the tradition of an Irish stew.

This dish came about through economic necessity, using cheap mutton, which was tough and required long, slow cooking, alongside the vegetables.

Add hard boiled eggs and a can of sweetcorn to a fish pie, or use salty meat like bacon or chopped sausages to flavour a rice or pasta dish. Meat doesn't have to be the star of the show, and can be used more as a garnish for less expensive ingredients.

Filling up on food like bread, potatoes and dumplings to stop you snacking on junk food, crisps, biscuits and chocolate is healthier as well as cheaper.

3 Eat less meat

Peasant food tends to use less meat, of course. If you really want to slash your food bill, eating more vegetarian food is a good way to do it.

There is plenty of research to suggest that a vegetarian or vegan diet can often be healthier, containing less fat and more fibre than the average Western diet. Increasingly, there is also a strong argument that eating less meat and dairy helps cut greenhouse emissions.

A 2018 study carried out by researchers at the University of Oxford, published in the journal *Science*, suggested that eating a vegan diet could reduce an individual's carbon footprint by as much as 73%.

If you can't sell the idea of a purely vegan, or even vegetarian, diet to your family, how about starting a Meat Free Monday? This idea has been around for a while now, but was popularised by the McCartney family (headed by Paul of the Beatles fame) when they started a campaign to encourage folk to, "help slow climate change, conserve precious natural resources and improve their health by having at least one plant-based day each week."

You can find inspiration for vegetarian and vegan food at the Meat Free Mondays website and at the Vegetarian Society.

4 Batch cooking

I have talked about how cooking mainly from scratch will save money on your food bill. However, it cannot be denied that it can take considerably more time. After all, that's what convenience food is all about.

Batch cooking is a way to get some of this time back. Cooking several meals in one go means fewer shopping trips, less time in the kitchen and the financial savings that come along with buying your ingredients in larger amounts. Batch cooking also saves on energy; you cook the food in one go initially and can later defrost and reheat it quickly in the microwave.

Some people choose to spend a day a month or a few hours each week in the kitchen batch cooking.

The easiest way to start batch cooking is to prepare bulk quantities of ingredients that can be used in a variety of meals. For example, minced beef fried up with onions could be a base for a cottage pie, bolognese sauce, chilli, etc.

You could batch cook and freeze large quantities of a basic tomato sauce, made with tomatoes, onions, garlic and herbs. This can later be added as it is to pasta with cheese, with lentils for a veggie bolognese, as a pizza topping or as the base for a lasagne, casserole or stew.

If you get serious about batch cooking, you can prepare and freeze all of your vegetables in advance to add to whatever meal you are making.

To keep it simple, I often just make a double quantity of whatever I am making in order to have a meal ready and portioned up for the following week.

The best way to store your batch-cooked food is flat in large zip lock bags. This way they take up far less space. Remember to always label and date them for stock control. However, old plastic takeaway containers, ice cream pots and so on would be a more eco-friendly option.

5 Yellow stickers

I tend to bang on about the importance of meal planning and sticking to a shopping list to save money and avoid food waste. However, there are times when I am flexible about this.

When I unexpectedly find food near its expiry date that has been reduced (or yellow-stickered), I will often buy it to store in the freezer or to incorporate into my meal plan in place of something else.

It pays to check that it is really a good reduction, though. Some retailers will drop items by 10 or 20p to begin with. The big reductions come at the end of the day or before a holiday, when you can pick up a loaf of bread for 10p, yoghurt for 25p, and various vegetables and meats for less than half price.

Sometimes I am just lucky to be there at the right time. Other times, I will make a special journey at, say, 3.30 on a Sunday afternoon, when it is likely the best bargains will be found.

Some people don't plan their meals at all and simply eat what they can find at a reduced price. A book I enjoyed a few years ago was by Kath Kelly, called *How I Lived a Year on Just a Pound a Day*. In order to meet her ambitious objective, she ate a lot of reduced food.

However, as many of the best reductions tend to be in the supermarket bakery aisle, she did put on weight!

A super scrimping blog I like to read is [Mean Queen, Life After Money](), written by Ilona, a pensioner who pretty much survives on yellow stickers. Nevertheless, she appears to eat a healthy, mostly vegetarian diet with a lot of fruit and vegetables.

Her philosophy on food goes as follows: "My eating habits are slightly unconventional. I don't follow recipes. I make my meals using whatever ingredients I have to hand. I am fairly flexible with what I eat. I only have three rules: it must be cheap, it must not be junk (no ready meals), and I do not eat meat. I mix things up that may not normally be served on the same plate - I like my food to be experimental."

This can mean eating a can of mushy peas with spaghetti, baked beans with carrots and potatoes, and lots of salads and raw vegetables. A diet like this would probably not suit you if you are feeding a family, but a single person can please themselves. She looks pretty healthy on it, for a woman in her seventies!

6 BOGOFs

I sometimes take advantage of BOGOFs (Buy One Get One Free offers) on non-perishable or freezable items, but only when I have checked that they are truly a good price.

This is because I have found BOGOFs, usually on more expensive branded items, that still work out more expensive than the supermarket's own version. I am also careful not to buy them unless I am confident we will use and enjoy them. It's not a bargain if your purchases sit in the cupboard for years gathering dust.

7 Coupons

I am aware that some people, particularly in America, get amazing reductions on food with the careful use of manufacturer coupons. However, in my experience, coupons tend to be offered on processed or junk food, rather than fresh, healthy produce.

I have occasionally found one for a brand of tea or coffee that I like, but generally I don't find them very useful.

If you are interested in saving money using coupons, I suggest you check out Jordon Cox, aka the Coupon Kid. Having worked out at the age of 15 how to save his single mum £100s on her grocery bill using coupons, he wrote a book called *Secrets to Saving, the Ultimate UK Couponing Guide* and now writes an all round money saving blog.

8 Go foraging

If you can't grow your own food, you can still go foraging. Even if you live in the city, it is possible to find food for free. If you use Instagram, check out John the Poacher.

He says, 'You can actually live off the land in London – mushrooms, berries, salads, it's all here. And trapping the odd rabbit on Hackney Marshes, of course'.

If the idea of trapping your own rabbits is a little extreme, you can always find some blackberries, add some dandelion leaves to your salad or scrump some apples.

The classic book on foraging is *Food For Free* by Richard Mabey, which gives advice on finding and cooking herbs, spices, roots, fruit, nuts, fungi and more.

9 Get free/cheap food and stop it being thrown away

There are some brilliant phone apps available aiming to prevent food waste. They enable you to pick food up for free or at least extremely cheaply.

Olio is my favourite. Every day individuals and businesses offer their excess food, as well as household items. Olio connects users in the local area so that they can advertise and collect food from people's homes, restaurants or shops.

It's a great way to help people out whilst reducing food waste. We are fortunate to have plenty of Olio Food Waste Heroes in our town, collecting waste food at the end of the day from retailers to give away via the Olio app. However, if you don't, then why not start one? There is information about how to do that on the Olio website.

Another good one is Too Good to Go, which offers 'magic bags' from local food retailers. You collect them near the end of the day for a fixed sum, usually between £3 and £5 at the time of writing, and you don't know what you will get until you pick it up. You can be sure that the price you pay will be just a fraction of what the full price would have been, however.

The description will tell you the types of items you might get and you can usually specify whether you want a vegetarian option.

You may also be lucky enough to have a community pantry or fridge in your area, where volunteers take waste food from various retailers that you can help yourself to.

MEAL PLANNING AND SHOPPING

I can't believe that once upon a time I never thought about meal planning. However, once I had discovered just how much time and money it saves me, I never looked back.

Meal planning saves money

If you buy too much food, you can end up throwing some of it away, as previously mentioned. If you buy too little, you are likely to find yourself making extra trips to the shops. You might then be tempted by more items than you actually need while you are there. The times I have done this and come out with an armful of chocolate or crisps....I have no willpower!

Meal planning helps you stick to your budget. If you have your whole week's food planned (or even your whole month's food for those of you who don't mind deciding that far ahead), you are far less likely to give into fast food, a takeaway or convenience meals on your way home from school or work.

Not that I am against convenience food *per se*. If you work full time and have a family, I can understand why you would happily cut corners when you need to. After all, a jar of pasta or casserole sauce is still much cheaper and easier on your budget than a takeaway.

Meal planning saves time

If you buy all the food you and your family are going to need in one go that will clearly save time. You can do a weekly shop and cut out all the extra trips you currently make because you have run out of cheese, fruit or whatever.

You won't be scratching your head when it comes to dinner time, trying to work out what to cook with some eggs and half a wilted cabbage. Your shopping list will be based on your plan and you will have all the ingredients you need for that day's meals.

You can factor in events that require you to produce a meal quickly. Maybe you are working late, need to cart children to swimming lessons, have a parents' evening or are off to the cinema. Planning ahead can also cut the stress of the hungry hoards moaning whilst you frantically rifle through the cupboards for a swift meal idea.

Meal planning helps prevent food waste

As you have probably noticed by the way I started my chapter on food with this topic, I hate wasting good food. You might as well throw your hard earned cash in the bin.

Meal planning means that you only purchase what you will eat during the course of the week. You are therefore less likely to let perishables spoil. When you check your cupboards to start your meal plan you can see what you have and use it up. You will avoid buying duplicates too.

Meal planning encourages healthy eating

When I was trying to lose weight, meal planning was essential. I was on a low fat diet and counting calories at the time. Having all of the ingredients needed for each meal really helped me to stick with my eating plan.

However, you don't need to be on a diet to find meal planning beneficial to your health. You can plan your nutritious meals for the week and be much less likely to splurge on processed or junk food. You can factor in some treats too. I actually think this is essential in order to stick to your plan and also your budget.

I always buy a bottle of wine, maybe a few packs of crisps or nuts, some dark chocolate or maybe some nice biscuits as a treat. We also enjoy lots of fruit, rye crackers and cheese.

We are realistic. If we don't allow ourselves some treats, we are much more likely to nip off to the corner shop and have a splurge! I do try to keep them pretty healthy though.

Where to start with meal planning

Begin by finding somewhere to write your plan. A chalk board or plain old piece of paper will do the job.

Next, check to see what you already have and which items have the shortest dates. Plan these into the meals you are going to make early in the week. Make sure you look in your fridge, freezer and cupboards.

I keep a folder of meals that I have found in magazines or printed off the Internet for inspiration. I also save interesting looking recipes on Pinterest.

Think about the week ahead. What are you going to be doing each day? Are you out in the evening? When do you need something quick and convenient and when will you have more time?

I tend to plan our evening meals, but have just a rough idea for lunches. I keep a stock of items in for those, such as eggs, rolls, canned sardines and tuna, home-made soups in the freezer, etc.

I don't bother planning for breakfast as it is nearly always porridge, fruit and yoghurt or toast.

If you are super-organised, however, you might like to plan every meal and all of your snacks.

Write a shopping list

Once you have planned your meals, you can write your shopping list. Most frugal folk will tell you to ALWAYS make a shopping list. Otherwise, as you hit the supermarket aisles, you tend to have conversations with yourself or your partner along the lines of, "Have we got any pasta? Not sure, let's get some just in case." Then you get home to find six packets of pasta lurking at the bottom of the cupboard with no space for the new lot....

Don't go food shopping when you are hungry

The other top tip before you head off to the supermarket is to have something to eat and drink. Going to the supermarket hungry skews your brain. Your belly will take over and the hunger pangs will rule what you take from the shelves rather than your budget!

As you can see, food is a hot topic when it comes to saving money and one of the most important areas to help you take and retain control of your finances.

Chapter 4: Granny's advice - 'Make do & Mend' and 'Waste Not, Want Not'

"Use it up, wear it out, make it do or do without." - The US War Advertising Council, 1944

The term 'makc do and mend' came from a WWII British government pamphlet, which featured tips for housewives for extending the life of clothing items and making new things from old.

Severe rationing meant that only two or three new items could be purchased in a year. As a result, clothes had to be handed down, made from scratch using whatever fabric people already had or repaired until they fell apart. Nothing could be wasted.

This particular pamphlet urged women to use their skills to unpick old jumpers and knit new items using the wool, to sew decorative patches onto worn elbows and knees, as well as darning and making alterations to the family's clothing.

Today, with an increasing emphasis on salvaging and recycling, we could learn a lot from the wartime generation.

DEVELOP YOUR SEWING SKILLS

Sadly, sewing is a life skill our schools no longer have time to teach. I am no seamstress, but I am old enough to have done needlework classes at school. As a result, I know how to repair a hem, sew on a button, patch a torn knee and mend a hole. This is a good bit of old fashioned frugality worth learning if you want to make your clothes last longer.

If you don't know how to thread a needle, let alone repair a rip in your trousers, get your older relatives to show you how, or look it up on YouTube.

This make do and mend attitude can extend to every aspect of your life. As mentioned previously, Mr Shoestring is very good at repairing stuff. He won't give in easily if something stops working and can often get most gizmos or gadgets going again.

Learning basic DIY and repair skills can save loads of money and extend the life of your belongings. Again, YouTube is a superb resource if you don't have a grandparent or great-grandparent to hand.

Good old fashioned frugality is about looking after what you have and valuing it, becoming more resourceful and doing stuff for yourself and, above all, not wasting anything.

Once you get into the mindset of stopping waste and saving money, it becomes second nature. For example, when I open a letter I place the empty envelope with my collection of scrap paper, to be used for writing notes and shopping lists. I keep old margarine and large yoghurt pots for storage. When we have leftovers we put them in these pots in the fridge or freezer to use as ready meals.

I remember our shoes lasting for ages as kids, because my dad would clean and polish them all once a week. We also paid to get them resoled and re-heeled if they needed it. They were good quality leather shoes and we made them last.

Some neighbours took this further by cutting out the toes of their children's shoes when they were getting a bit snug, converting them to sandals! This may be a step too far for most of us, but buying some shoe polish and shoe brushes will be a worthwhile investment.

Other useful pieces of kit are a clothes brush and a fabric shaver to keep your clothing looking good. I have found both of these very helpful to liven up an old jumper or to remove the bobbles that tend to accumulate on cotton tops.

My Facebook group, My Second Hand & Frugal Life, has many examples of people's ingenuity in making do and mending. Members darn socks to make them last for years, turn their daughters' favourite dresses into skirts and scrunchies when they outgrow them and mend holes in trousers with humour, sewing eyes and teeth onto patched knees!

Extending the life of your clothing means you can buy fewer items and less will go to landfill. But you don't have to stop at clothing.

ESSENTIAL MAINTENANCE AND HOW TO MAKE THINGS LAST

Maintaining and looking after your possessions, be they household appliances, furniture, carpets, vehicles or bicycles will keep them looking good and remaining usable for longer.

For example:

1 Hairdryers. If you use your hairdryer on full power every time, you will be lucky if it lasts a year. I get four to five years of use from mine, used every other day, by selecting the lower power option.

2 Razors. If you wash and dry your razor after each use, you will need to replace the blades far less often.

3 Refrigerators. Vacuum or dust the compressor coils at the back of your fridge every few months. The compressor is an expensive part to replace and if it is clean it doesn't have to work as hard to dissipate the heat from your appliance. This also saves on energy.

4 Towels, clothing and bed linen. The less often you wash things, the longer they will last. Line dry rather than tumble dry if possible. This is better for the fabric and will save on energy too. Consider dying faded towels and linen rather than replacing them.

5 Spectacles and sunglasses. If the arms fall off an expensive pair of specs or even non-prescription sunglasses, your optician will usually fix them for free. I have found this to be the case even if I didn't purchase the glasses from them in the first place.

6 Get your boiler serviced regularly. Keeping your gas boiler running optimally will make it more efficient, ensure you are safe from gas leaks and keep it running well for many years.

7 Fix your appliances. I do find it depressing that it is often as cheap to buy a new appliance like a washing machine as it is to repair an old one. However, I have come across many stories of people buying parts and fixing things themselves, using books and YouTube videos.

It is worth noting that if you purchase a quality appliance in the first place, it will definitely be worth the initial extra expense, as it will last longer and thus save money in the long run.

8 Microwaves. I have learned the hard way that if you shut your microwave door when it is full of condensation, the inside will begin to rust. This makes your microwave unsafe. After each use, wipe down the interior and leave the door ajar for five minutes or so.

9 Clean and maintain your washing machine. Make sure you clean the filter on your washing machine regularly. Scrub the detergent drawer every few weeks with a bottle brush and some white vinegar. Rub around the drum and make sure you clean around the rubber door seal thoroughly. Use some washing up liquid if the dirt doesn't come off easily.

Run the machine without a load once a month with 500g of soda crystals. This will clean the machine and prevent limescale build up. If you live in a very hard water area, use 250g of citric acid every other month to keep your machine clean, free of limescale and prevent bad smells developing.

10 Clean and maintain your dishwasher. Wipe the doors and rim of your dishwasher with white vinegar or liquid soda crystals and hot water. Empty and wash the filter and check that there is nothing caught in the well of the filter.

Dri-pak, who manufacture soda crystals, do not recommend that you clean this appliance with them. Instead, they suggest dissolving two tablespoons of citric acid in two bowls and placing one on the top shelf and one on the bottom shelf of your machine. Then run an intensive cycle.

11 Clean and maintain your tumble dryer. Personally, I don't own a tumble dryer. It's more economical and eco-friendly to line dry washing. However, if you have a house full of people in the depths of winter, I can understand why a tumble dryer would be preferable to clothes airers constantly full of wet laundry.

According to *Which?*, the best ways to keep your tumble dryer running well are as follows:

Clean the lint filter after every use; If you have a condenser dryer, empty the tank after each use; Clean the heat exchanger on your machine regularly. A build-up of dust and fibres slows the flow of air and makes the tumble dryer less efficient; Regularly clean the inside of the drum and the drying sensor.

12 Carpets. The best way to keep your carpets looking new is to keep the dirt outside. Have a policy to remove shoes in the hallway. Keep a towel by the door to clean and dry the dog's paws too.

Vacuum regularly, and deal with stains immediately, before they have time to sink into the carpet fibres.

If a section of your carpet becomes damaged, replace just that piece if you have to. There are some good tutorials on YouTube showing you how to repair or replace small areas of your carpet.

REUSING AND REPURPOSING

"We really never, never threw anything away. You think you know about recycling? We invented it. We had to. We were desperate." - Clara Cannucciari on living through the Great Depression

As I said previously, our recent ancestors would have baulked at some of the things that we carelessly discard. If you visit any landfill site, you will find people throwing away working electrical items, perfectly usable furniture, toys, kitchen equipment, clothing and more.

However, by reusing and repurposing, you not only extend the life of an item and save it from landfill, you will also need to spend a lot less on new things.

Before you throw anything away, ask yourself a simple question, 'Could I use this for anything else?' This one question could save you a lot of money, as well as enabling you to live more sustainably.

Going back to Sarah Lazarovic's Buyerarchy of Needs, remember that the bottom layer of her pyramid for sustainable living - the largest section - recommends that we use what we already have.

I'm not suggesting that you become a hoarder, and keep every glass jar, piece of wood or plastic bag that comes your way. Most of us simply don't have the space. But it is a good ploy to foresee what you might need in the future, and begin to think creatively about your belongings before you dispose of them.

Here are just a few ideas to reuse or repurpose:

1 All sorts of containers can be used to pot up plants and grow seeds. Cardboard toilet roll tubes make great little biodegradable seed pots, for example. The tough plastic trays that mushrooms come in are good seed trays too. Just make a few small holes in the bottom for drainage.

2 Plastic containers from products like ice cream and margarine can be reused to store leftovers, take your packed lunch to work or school, to keep your needlework equipment in, to organise your nails and screws, etc. You can even make them pretty by painting them or covering them in fabric or sticky back plastic.

3 Old glass jars can be used in a similar way for storage. I save the larger ones (especially coffee containers with glass lids) to keep our pasta, rice, cereals and pulses in, for example.

4 Empty jam jars look beautiful with tea lights in them. Wrap some twine around the rims and hang them decoratively from fences and trees in your garden when you are entertaining.

5 Ditch kitchen roll and disposable wipes. Instead save old T-shirts and towels, cut into squares and store in an old box or jar to use as dishcloths, to mop up spillages and for general cleaning. I find these so much more absorbent than squares of paper. They go straight into the washing machine after use to be cleaned in the next load.

6 Keep lemon and orange peels to make cleaning products. See Chapter 8 for more information on frugal cleaning.

7 If you need to replace windows or glass doors, the old ones can be repurposed by propping them against a fence to make a cold frame for your seedlings. Make sure the glass is intact and safe.

8 Before you discard your old fridge, take out the clear plastic vegetable drawers. These also make good mini cold frames. Alternatively, you might be able to sell them. My daughter wanted to replace her vegetable drawer and found that as a spare part from the manufacturer it was going to cost £50!

9 Keep old pieces of foil, ribbon, sweet wrappers, fabric, card, string, toilet roll tubes, etc. to entertain your children, instead of buying expensive craft kits. Give them some glue and scissors, and let them get creative.

10 Retain the return envelopes you often receive from your bank and in charity junk mail and use them. Just stick a label over the address.

11 It's also worth saving a few of the small cardboard boxes you get from online retailers. Simply flatten them so that they don't take up much storage space. If you go into the Post Office and purchase a box, they can be surprisingly expensive.

12 Jiffy bags are another item that you need never purchase new, as they can be used again and again.

13 Gardeners love old tights for storing produce such as onions, or as plant ties.

14 If you don't want to invest in a fabric shaver to debobble your clothing, try using an old disposable razor instead.

15 Old lemonade or milk bottles can be filled with sand and used as weights for your home work out.

16 Plastic bottles and old colanders can also be repurposed as bird feeders.

17 The strong plastic bags that your cereal arrives in are too good to throw away without reusing. I wash mine with the dishes and hang them upside down to dry. Bread and fruit bags also get reused several times, but only once for meat or fish items.

18 When you get new tyres on your car, ask to take away the old ones. They make nice planters and can even be painted to suit your colour scheme.

19 Old CDs or DVDs can be tied around your vegetable patch to scare away the birds. They can also be painted bright colours and hung on ribbons or twine as outdoor Christmas decorations.

20 Get into upcycling furniture. Solid pieces, even if they are quite old-fashioned, can be transformed with some decent paint. A great source of inspiration for this is the Frenchic Fan Forum group on Facebook.

When you start to question yourself before you dispose of anything - even if it is recyclable - you will find you get your creative juices flowing, save some money and give yourself a warm, green glow of achievement that your grandma would be proud of.

Chapter 5: Buying Second-Hand and Getting Everything for Less

"I get high to be totally honest, in second-hand shops. My hunting instinct, I expect, really kicks in." - Bjork

They say the best things in life are free and to a large extent that is true. The things I truly value - my family and friends - are there no matter how much is in my bank account. I am grateful!

However, we live in a world where we require money for many of the things we need and the activities we want to do. It is also true, though, that with a bit of thought and creativity you can get hold of a lot of great stuff and experiences really cheaply and sometimes even for free.

BUYING SECOND-HAND

Buying second-hand 90% of the time is probably our biggest money saver. One of the reasons I like to buy second-hand - besides saving money and the planet - is that it generally means I can buy better quality at a low price.

We have all bought cheap and regretted it. When you need something new and can't find it second-hand, be it a pair of shoes or a washing machine, try to buy the best quality you can afford. Cheap new items are often shoddy and not made to last.

As I sit here on my second-hand sofa bed (free, from Mr Shoestring's brother), I can see more items of furniture that were pre-loved than were new.

There are many reasons I like buying second-hand. Most importantly, when you are on a tight budget, second-hand items are cheaper. If you need to save money, it makes sense to pay less for things when you can.

Living a second-hand life means that you can help develop a circular economy, where items are produced and used until the end of their lives. Perhaps they may be repaired and upcycled along the way, rather than discarded when the owner is bored with them and fancies a change. You get the maximum value from each item and can then recycle or reuse as much as possible of what remains.

Here are some of my favourite second-hand items.

My Windsor armchair

We have a beautiful old Windsor arm chair in our living room. It is more than just second-hand; it is an antique, given to me by a family member more than 20 years ago, having previously been passed down from her grandmother.

It has been in several houses since I got it, fitting in beautifully with the shabby chic style I favour, and I love it! I purchased a gorgeous crochet cushion recently to spruce it up.

Welsh dresser

In the kitchen, we have a small wooden Welsh dresser. This is another piece that has been passed through the family. My parents had it made in a honey-coloured pine in the late seventies, to go with the honey coloured pine kitchen that my dad made from scratch (all the rage at the time!).

I had it in my first home, as my parents no longer needed it and it was small enough to fit into a snug two-bed terrace. It has come with me ever since, was at one point a Brittany blue, but is now a sage green.

It is crammed with vintage mismatched china, all from junk shops. There is nothing of any great value, but it gives an appealing shabby chic vibe!

Wicker vase

I recently found a large vase encased in wicker at a boot sale for £2. The seller told me regretfully that she had paid £30 for it in a smart store, but it didn't go with her current decor.

It looks fabulously retro with some dried pampas grass in it.

Sofas

We have pets, and have a relaxed approach about living with them. We are also more than happy to have them sitting on our laps on the sofa. As a result, we don't buy expensive furniture, especially anything upholstered.

In our sitting room we have two second-hand sofas. One came from Mr S's brother, as I mentioned already, who was given it for free but didn't use it. The bonus is that it is also a very comfortable pull out bed, which is great when we have visitors.

The other was from a local charity shop and has removable, washable covers.

A retro reading lamp

I absolutely love our large, retro reading lamp, which was in a pile of things a friend was giving away after a house move. I was shocked to find that lamps like this cost upwards of £100 purchased new.

My wheels

I have never bought a new car in my life, and I am pretty sure I never will. They lose so much value as soon as they are driven off the forecourt. A car purchase is certainly not an investment, unless you are buying vintage!

I suppose someone has to buy them new, but I will leave that for others with deeper pockets.

When you buy a used car, it is better, if you possibly can, to save up and pay cash, avoiding debt and the accompanying interest payments. You can also read the reviews and avoid common problems with particular models. Somebody else has done the testing and ironed out the issues.

Our 'best' dinner service

My mum picked up a beautiful vintage china dinner service for me a decade ago, and it is still going strong. It was a fraction of the price of a new service of similar quality.

Although I am generally not a fan of saving anything 'for best', this does only come out when we have dinner guests. The rest of the time, we use thrifted and mismatched cups, plates and bowls.

So, the next time you need something, rather than going straight for something new, check out second-hand and antique stores, classified ads and some of the online sites.

WHERE TO FIND SECOND-HAND BARGAINS

Here are some good places to purchase pre-loved items online:

Gumtree - you can find pretty much anything on Gumtree, from cars to clothing, furniture to garden tools.

Schpock - Schpock sells itself as 'the boot sale app'. However, you can find more than you would at your average boot sale and can buy most things via the app. You can set your search to exclude new items.

Preloved - Like Gumtree and Schpock, you will find ads for anything the average householder could possibly need.

eBay - eBay sells pretty much everything internationally. You can set your search filters to show you used items.

Oxfam Online – This site sells all of the items you would typically find in an Oxfam shop: clothing, homeware, books and music, plus collectibles. However, this is one of the most expensive charity shops, and their online collection tends to be higher end and vintage items.

Depop - This is aimed at the young and trendy, listing designer, high end branded and vintage fashion, plus streetwear. I feel it is quite expensive.

Vinted - Great for well-priced second-hand clothing, shoes and accessories.

Secondhand.org.uk - This brings several of these sites together in one place, so is also worth checking out as a one-stop shop.

Facebook Marketplace - Another way to find used items for sale locally is Marketplace. I have noticed that more and more new stuff is appearing there too. However, it isn't regulated in the same way as, say, eBay is. I have heard of people paying in advance for items that didn't turn up. One of my Facebook group members also sold a games console and was given cash, which turned out to be fake. It can be good, but proceed with caution with higher value items.

It is also worth a search of your local charity shops as many of them have created online shops for their high end items. However, you will be charged more for these.

A SECOND-HAND CASE STUDY

Another member of my Facebook group, Caroline Anderson, along with husband Jay, made a stunning bathroom sink out of an old copper hot water tank.

Their thrifty creativity has also seen them carpet their stairs with a patchwork of samples from their local carpet shop. Not only does this look quirky and original, it has the advantage that individual samples can be swapped out if they become worn or damaged.

There is very little in Caroline and Jay's house that was purchased new. Even their kitchen is made from other people's cast offs. They have a section made from an old Welsh dresser top, glass from a 1920s door, a mosaic splashback created from scavenged second-hand tiles and a beautiful oak floor, made from rescued pieces that were going to be burnt as firewood. Theirs is a unique, comfortable and interesting home created on a shoestring budget.

FINDING STUFF FOR FREE

A quick internet search will introduce you to a whole world of freebies. There are many sites pointing you to companies and brands keen to get your attention.

Usually, they require you to sign up to a newsletter, catalogue, take part in a survey or download their app, and in return will give you a voucher, sample or gift. Sometimes you can receive trial products for the price of the postage only.

It is also possible to get free tester samples in return for your feedback.

The downsides

One downside of getting freebies in this way is that you tend to get bombarded with digital junk mail. If you plan to go freebie foraging on a regular basis, I suggest setting up an email box specifically for the purpose.

Another is that you will usually receive small samples with quite a lot of packaging, which isn't ideal if you are trying to live more sustainably.

That said, free samples of cosmetics, perfume, confectionery, etc can be good additions to your ongoing gift collection and make great stocking fillers at Christmas.

Where to find freebies online

Good websites to investigate for freebies in the UK are latestdeals.co.uk, magicfreebies.co.uk and freestuff.com.

If you are outside of the UK, an internet search for 'freebies' plus the name of your home country should provide similar results.

You can also apply to test new products, which you get to keep. Some sites that offer this opportunity are hometesterclub.com, clicksresearch.com and bzzagent.com. You don't always get chosen for every campaign, so bear that in mind.

Find free stuff locally

Another great way to find freebies is to join your local Freecycle or Freegle group. Both organisations were set up with the intention to encourage reuse and prevent stuff ending up in landfill.

It also saves you the trouble of taking items you no longer need to the landfill site or charity shop, as people will happily collect from you.

Over the years, we have picked up clothing, furniture, a freezer, a cat bed and plants. We have also got rid of old cabinet doors, an exercise bike, excess seeds and plants, and a roof rack.

The Trash Nothing app brings groups like this together, so is worth downloading if you want to keep it simple.

I have also found Facebook Marketplace good for getting rid of things we don't want and picking up free items from time to time.

Skip diving

You can find some amazing discarded items for free from skips outside people's homes, as well as shops and businesses.

We once fished out some fabulous, top-quality plates and bowls from a skip in front of a restaurant that was being refurbished. We couldn't believe our eyes once we began to search. There were boxes and boxes of completely new crockery! We took as many as we could carry, being some distance from our car, but once other passers-by saw what we had found they began to jump in and help themselves.

I heard of a man recently who gets all of the wood for his wood burner from skips and barely uses his gas central heating boiler as a result. Other skip divers I know have found useful DIY materials, furniture, mugs, garden chairs and toys. One lady even came across a haul of working power tools!

It is recommended that you should always ask before taking items from skips and don't enter private property without permission.

Having said that, there are people, often known as 'Freegans', who will happily sneak into the skips behind shops and take anything usable, including food. In his book, *The Moneyless Man*, Mark Boyle wrote about his experience as a supermarket bin raider:

"Most nights we'd find anywhere between ten and twenty loaves of bread, and stumbling on cases of fruit and vegetables was far too common."

He also found full cases of wine, discarded because one broken bottle had made the others unsaleable, and a case of condoms which had been thrown out because the packaging was water damaged. Sounds like a good (free) night in!

Although it is unlikely that a business would prosecute you for rooting through their bins, strictly speaking it is illegal and they could press a charge of trespass or even theft.

Freebies within your community

A safer option is to look out for freebies within your local community. We often find that neighbours have put unwanted items from their decluttering efforts onto the street in front of their houses. Look out for the FREE signs!

We have picked up bric-a-brac, almost full pots of paint and once, memorably, a garden bench, which we had fun walking down the road to our garden.

Children's toys pop up a lot on freebie tables, so have a walk around your neighbourhood some time and see what is available.

It's a very effective way of getting rid of your own stuff too. Even though every year I swear I won't grow too many seedlings, I invariably do. Rather than throw them away, I leave them in the front garden for my neighbours and passers-by to take.

Sending compliments

Most of us will have sent the odd stiff letter or email of complaint to businesses complaining about poor service or shoddy products. However, sending a compliment instead can get you some generous freebies.

I tested this out by sending an email to a well-known cat food manufacturer to tell them how much my cats were enjoying their products. To my complete astonishment, they sent me a thank you in the form of £10 worth of free vouchers!

It won't work every time, but if you have a few minutes to spare, why not give it a try?

COMPETITIONS AND CASHBACK SITES

Competitions

If you want a challenging hobby that can reap fantastic rewards, how about entering some competitions?

An old work colleague of mine spends one hour every evening entering any competitions he comes across. He has at least one free holiday pretty much every year, and wins prizes constantly! It is like a second income to him, and well worth the investment of his time.

Again, it is wise to set up a special email address for competitions, as you will receive a lot of spam as a result. Don't forget to check it regularly in case you win, though.

Good sites for finding competitions are Super Lucky Me, Loquax and The Prize Hub, as well as the competition thread on the forum at moneysavingexpert.com.

Cashback sites

Cashback sites won't get you freebies or discounts. However, they do exactly what you would imagine from their title - they give you cash back on your online shopping. This can add up to a considerable amount, especially at those times you can't avoid spending a bit more than usual, such as Christmas.

Whenever you make an online purchase, don't forget to see if the merchant you are buying from is on a cashback site. This is money for free!

You can get cash back on so many things, from switching your utilities or buying a holiday, to banking, buying clothes or shopping for homeware.

Good cashback sites to try are TopCashBack and Quidco.

If you want to be frugal like your grandma and get top value for your money, buy second-hand, get stuff for free and, where you do need to pay full price, at least get cash back.

Chapter 6: Slashing Your Monthly Bills

"Energy consumption matters to both our environment and our economy." - John Baldacci

REDUCING YOUR ENERGY BILLS

Like everyone else, I am concerned about the ever-increasing cost of our energy bills. Gas and electricity combined make up one of our biggest monthly outgoings. As a result, I am always on the lookout for ways to reduce the amount we have to pay. I have found that there are some simple steps that you can take if you want to save money and benefit the environment.

We choose to use a green energy tariff, which is slightly more expensive than a standard tariff. However, it is important to us that our energy is from an eco-friendly source. Paying more for our green energy means that it is even more important not to waste any.

Here are some suggestions to help cut your energy bills.

1 Look at your light bulbs

Invest in LED energy saving bulbs. They are more expensive to buy, but considerably cheaper to run than halogen bulbs. *Which?* estimates that an LED bulb costs about £1.71 to run annually, as opposed to £8.42 for a halogen equivalent.

2 Go for a cooler wash

Try a cooler, shorter wash when doing the laundry. A 30-degree, 30-minute wash will still clean most averagely-grubby clothes effectively, and your clothes will fade less and last longer.

3 Line dry

Use airers to dry your laundry or, best of all, hang outside on a sunny day. We invested in a heated airer and also a dehumidifier to help dry the laundry in the winter. They are both very effective and cost less to run than a tumble dryer.

4 Check your tariff

If you have a large family and not much space, the idea of drying clothes in the winter without a tumble dryer may seem distinctly unappealing. Consider whether a cheaper night time tariff might be a good option for you, then invest in a timer to run as many electrical items overnight as possible.

5 Fill up the dishwasher

Don't run the dishwasher unless it is full. We use ours most days and have invested in an energy efficient model. It may be slightly cheaper to wash your dishes by hand, but there is also an argument that dishwashers can be more sustainable, using less energy, water and detergent.

6 Turn it off

Go round the house and turn off everything at the plug that is left on standby. Culprits in many homes are phone chargers plugged in at the wall and TVs manufactured with no off button. Don't forget laptops, printers and PCs when they are not in use.

Similarly, train your family to do all of the above and turn off the light when they leave a room unoccupied.

7 Boil only the water you need

When you use the kettle, only boil the water you need. If you do boil more, stick it in a thermos and use it later.

8 Buy for energy efficiency

Buy energy saving appliances. This is tricky if you have to buy second-hand, but not impossible if you do some research in advance. The last appliance I purchased was a large fridge freezer, which is triple A rated for energy efficiency.

9 Invest in a condensing boiler

Condensing boilers have a high energy efficiency rate of over 90%, which can lower your energy bills by £200 yearly if your current boiler is non-condensing.

However, I wouldn't replace your boiler until it absolutely needs it. They are an expensive investment.

10 Get the best deal

Shop around to see if you can find a better deal on your energy provider and if you can fix your tariff. I recommend starting by reading the Money Saving Expert website as a starting point*.

*(*As I write this, energy prices in the UK are so high that it's almost impossible to get a good fix that will save you money, so approach with caution.)*

11 Have a shower rather than a bath

Showering rather than bathing will generally use a lot less hot water, which means you can adjust your timer and heat the boiler for less time. However, this isn't necessarily the case if you have a power shower, as they can use as much hot water as a bath. Set a timer on your phone to see how long you spend in the shower on average, then challenge yourself to be quicker.

If you prefer to take a bath, share your water with another member of the household. Kids can all pile in together!

12 Turn down the water temperature

You could also consider turning down the water temperature by adjusting the thermostat on your boiler. I did this by one degree and nobody noticed the difference.

13 Turn down the heating thermostat

Turn down your general thermostat to no more than 21 degrees. The Energy Saving Trust estimates that just one degree lower could save £65 a year.

14 Don't heat unused rooms

If you are lucky enough to have a spare room, turn off the radiator when you have no guests and close the door.

15 Insulate

Insulate your loft and wall cavities. We had ours done for free with British Gas. Check with your energy supplier to see what they offer.

If you are in receipt of certain benefits you may be entitled to insulation and a new boiler, even if you don't own your property. If you are UK based, check the gov.uk website for current availability.

16 Cut the draughts

Use draught excluders at the bottom of your doors and fit extra linings to your curtains.

Consider fitting reflective radiator foil behind your radiators. We have done this in a few rooms and really noticed the difference.

17 Use your oven efficiently

If you have your oven on, can you cook something else at the same time? How about flapjacks for the lunchboxes whilst you are doing tonight's casserole? Fill your oven up when you use it.

Alternatively, use less energy hungry means to cook. Slow cookers, air fryers, pressure cookers and microwaves are cheaper to run.

18 Don't auto renew

It pays to shop around regularly to see if you can get a better deal and then fix your tariff for a year.

If you want to take the effort out of this, you could consider signing up with a company such as Look After My Bills, who automatically switch you to the cheapest provider each year.

19 Get a smart meter

If you haven't already, request a smart meter from your energy provider. They show you how much gas and electricity you are using day-to-day with a breakdown of the cost. Seeing this every day makes you hyper aware of usage. We keep our monitor in the kitchen where we can all see it.

REDUCING YOUR WATER BILL

We tend to take our clean and plentiful water supply for granted. However, when you consider that many people in developing countries don't have access to clean water and that climate change poses a potential threat to our future water supplies, reducing the amount you use is not just about saving money.

There are many small steps that you can take to reduce your household's water usage. Here are some ideas.

1 Install a water meter

Installing a water meter can make you more conscious about the amount you use. However, when I had three teenage girls at home I resisted. Since you pay for what you use with a meter, I decided that a flat rate was probably cheaper. Once they left, we moved to a meter and cut our bill in half!

Make sure you register for an online account with your water supplier so that you can monitor your household's use. It is very enlightening. I was surprised at how much our water use shot up in the summer when we watered the garden, for example.

2 Shower rather than bath

As I mentioned in the previous section about reducing your energy usage, choosing a shower rather than a bath is generally a better option if you want to reduce your water bill.

As I said before, it is worth noting that power showers can use as much water (and energy) as having a bath.

3 Shower less

Whilst I am not suggesting you allow yourself to get smelly, you could consider whether you need to bathe or shower every day. Many people manage with a strip wash over a sink full of water instead.

4 Turn off taps

Don't leave the tap running when you clean your teeth. Similarly, run a bowl full of water to wash up, rather than cleaning mugs, etc under a running tap. Only run as much water as you require for the task.

5 If it's yellow…

Save water by not flushing unless you do a 'number two'. Controversial I know, but you will save water if you live by the maxim: "If it's yellow, let it mellow. If it's brown, flush it down!"

6 Fill it up

As mentioned in the energy saving section, if you have a dishwasher, make sure it is full before you run it. Do the same with your washing machine.

7 Install water butts

Try to avoid using a hose to water the garden. Instead, make sure you have water butts installed to collect rainwater. Plants prefer this anyway.

You can also collect some of the 'grey water' from your shower or bath and use this in the garden. However, this doesn't store well and will quickly become smelly, so use it up quickly.

8 Save water when flushing

Place a cistern displacement device (CDD) in your cistern. This can save around a litre of water per flush. Your water company will usually give you a CDD free of charge.

9 Install water efficient taps and toilets

If you fit a new toilet, try to purchase a water efficient one. Similarly, you could consider installing low flow showers and taps to reduce your water use.

10 Report any leaks

If you suspect that you have a water leak, report it to your supplier straight away.

COUNCIL TAX

Council tax forms a considerable lump of most household's outgoings in the UK. As it is set by your local authority, you won't have much control over how much you have to pay.

However, there are some things to consider, particularly if you are on a low income.

1 Claim discounts

If you are the only adult in the home, you can claim a 25% discount on your bill. Over 18s in full time education do not affect this.

If all adults in the home are full time students, you do not have to pay council tax.

You may also receive a discount if you have a physical or severe mental disability.

Check the gov.uk website for details of potential reductions to your council tax bill or speak to your local authority.

2 Check your home is in the correct banding

According to Money Saving Expert, hundreds of thousands of homes in the UK were placed into the wrong band when the current system was put in place in the early 1990s. The MSE site gives step by step instructions on how to find out and claim money back if you are entitled. Some people have been awarded thousands of pounds using this method.

BROADBAND AND TV

Broadband with a TV and phone package can be a significant expense. Most of us can't survive without an internet connection these days, but do we really need all those TV channels?

If you need to save money, consider other options. When we were streamlining our finances, we opted for a broadband only package and got rid of our landline. The only calls we ever seemed to receive at home were of the sales or nuisance variety anyway!

As we don't often go to pubs and restaurants, the theatre or the cinema, we watch TV quite often. However, we found that a Freeview box offered a good variety of programmes. We have yet to invest in a smart TV, but discovered that an Amazon Firestick was a useful interim purchase. It allows us to stream audio and video content from dozens of different apps over our Wi-Fi connection. There are other similar gadgets available from the likes of Apple and Roku. Do your research before purchasing.

We also found Netflix was a worthwhile monthly expense. These three things combined give us as much TV as we can possibly consume at a much cheaper price than previous satellite and cable packages have. Plus, we aren't tied into any contracts.

Whichever option you go for, shop around for the best deal, and make sure you renegotiate at the end of your contract. Suppliers are likely to hike the price up once any promotional period has finished. At this point, if you threaten to leave, their retention department will be happy to give you a much better deal.

To sum up, be aware of what you are spending on utilities and any other regular monthly bills, get the best deal by shopping around and take measures to use less and make your home as efficient as possible.

Chapter 7: Making a Frugal Home

"There is no place like home." L. Frank Baum

Living somewhere you like and making a warm and comfortable home is crucial to a good quality of life. Fortunately, most of us don't require five-star luxury and it is more than possible to have a lovely home on a budget.

Here are some ideas to keep your housing costs low, to furnish and decorate without breaking the bank and even some ways to make money from your home.

REDUCING YOUR HOUSING COSTS

Housing is a huge expense for many of us. Unless you still live with your parents or other family members, your mortgage or rent could take up to 40% of your monthly income (although ideally, not more than 30%).

Keeping your housing costs as low as possible makes sense if you are on a tight budget or if you are saving for a specific goal. But how can you do that without compromising on comfort and safety?

Here are some ideas to help you pay your rent or mortgage.

1 Downsize

Firstly, if you are struggling with your payments, consider downsizing or moving to a cheaper area.

Don't be a postcode snob! For example, we currently live in an ex-local authority 1940s semi-detached property, set in a quiet leafy street. Half a mile up the road, houses of a similar size and style can cost £50,000 more to purchase, purely because they weren't built as social housing. Similarly, you can expect to pay around £200 per month more for a rental in a 'better' area.

2 Think tiny

The tiny house movement is the ultimate in downsizing, offering affordable, eco-friendly housing for those looking to reduce their housing costs and live more simply.

A tiny home is defined as having a floor area of less than 37 square metres, or 400 square feet. Their size means that they naturally have far lower energy costs and are frequently designed to be off grid.

However, although they offer a good alternative for singletons looking to downsize, they perhaps aren't the ideal space for growing families. You also have to find suitable land to situate your tiny home.

Some beautiful examples of tiny houses can be found at Tiny House UK.

3 Become a property guardian

There are ways to find somewhere to live much more cheaply. An idea that can work well if you live in a city is to become a property guardian through a social enterprise such as Dot Dot Dot. They make renting in London and other cities more affordable by matching empty buildings with guardians. The catch, if you can call it that, is that you have to volunteer for 16 hours a month at a charity of your choice. Dot Dot Dot states:

"On behalf of owners, we take good care of buildings that would otherwise be empty. We provide guardians with good quality housing which is much more cost effective than the private rental market. And we make a positive difference to communities by ensuring our guardians are great neighbours who volunteer for good causes while preventing the blight that empty buildings cause."

Be aware of the pitfalls of property guardianship, however. Some unscrupulous companies have been accused of offering substandard accommodation whilst milking the system to pay less tax. Read the small print and be aware of what you are taking on and your rights as a licensee.

4 Get a lodger

You could also help cover the cost of your mortgage by renting a spare room, if you have one, to a lodger. We have done this for many years very successfully.

In the UK, you can earn up to a threshold of £7,500 per year tax-free from letting out furnished accommodation in your home

(2022). Find out more about the Rent a Room Scheme at gov.uk.

Be very clear about which rooms your lodger can use, whether the kitchen equipment is shared or if they need to provide their own, whether bedding and bed linen is included, etc.

Ask for references from previous landlords if at all possible or request an employer reference. We always ask for one month's rent in advance and a small damage deposit.

Draw up a lodger agreement stating the amount and date the rent should be paid, the required amount of notice on each side, the deposit amount, etc.

Spareroom.com is a good place to advertise your room for free, and also has a basic lodger agreement that you can purchase for a small fee.

5 Host foreign language students

If you don't want a full-time lodger, you could consider hosting foreign students some of the time. Many towns have language schools or organisations that provide learning holidays for young people.

We hosted students on and off for almost eight years. During that time we met great people from all over the world.

We are lucky to have an English Study Centre where we live. Obviously not every town will have one. Do some research on the internet to see which organisations teach English as a Foreign Language as they may require host families.

You will find some organisations that recruit host families in the References section of this book.

6 Offer B&B

Another option to make occasional income from your home is to sign up with an organisation such as Airbnb.

You can rent out your spare space for one night or several weeks. The most basic requirement is a comfortable, clean sleeping space and access to a bathroom.

Airbnb works well if you live in a tourist area. You will need to promote your home with a great description, but it's important to be honest and set expectations realistically. If you live in the middle of a city, what might be exciting and bustling to some guests may be stressful and noisy to others.

Another option if you live in a location with a theatre is the Theatre Digs Booker website. Fancy offering a room to an actor, darling?

Things to consider when you are renting out a room

If you are renting out a spare room, whether to a lodger, language student or B&B guest, it is important to check with your mortgage provider or freeholder that it is allowed first. If you are a tenant, you will need to check with your own landlord.

Also, make sure any theft or damage will be covered and that you have adequate public liability cover by speaking to your insurance provider.

7 Get a job with accommodation

Recently spotted in the *The Lady* magazine: "Live-in couple required for housekeeping, driving and gardening duties in a French chateau. Three-bedroom cottage available, stables and riding facility available. Must speak French."

This French idyll sounds like the ideal career to keep your housing costs to the minimum. However, I know from my own parents, who undertook a similar role a few decades ago in a manor house in Norfolk, that this type of role can mean you are on call 24 hours a day and is extremely hard work. The salary itself is also likely to be very low.

Another downside is that if you want to change careers or lose your job for some reason, you also lose your home.

That said, a job with accommodation will appeal to some. Here are some jobs that frequently come with housing:

Nanny/au pair

Carer/companion

Independent school matron

Housekeeper/cook/gardener (often these roles require a couple)

Some hotels also offer discounted accommodation for staff.

MAKING THE BEST OF YOUR HOME ON A BUDGET

If you slavishly follow trends when it comes to home decor, every few years you will feel impelled to redecorate as you feel rooms begin to look jaded and old-fashioned.

On the other hand, choosing timeless styles that you truly like will mean that your classically decorated home looks great for years.

Putting fashion aside, what *is* your style? What are the types of rooms that always make you feel good and comfortable? Are there colours and patterns that you are drawn to again and again?

For example, I like lots of light, so I prefer to paint walls and woodwork with neutral colours. These neutrals just don't date.

In my teens, I loved the look the furniture shop Habitat was known for: clean, comfortable and neutral, with simple, quality furniture, plus lots of plants, bright cushions, rugs and throws to add some colour and individuality. Now, 40 plus years later, I continue to find that look contemporary and appealing. It still works!

You could save a lot of money in the long run by giving some thought to what you really like rather than what the glossy magazines tell you is a must for your home this season.

Remember - if you don't love it, don't buy it. Even if an item is the best bargain in the world, if it's not exactly what you want and need you will just want to change it in the short term.

Learning DIY

Another way to create a beautiful home on a budget is to do a lot of the work yourself.

A good starting point is to teach yourself some painting and wallpaper skills, but why stop there? You can learn tiling, basic plastering, carpet laying, how to put up a shelf, build flat pack furniture and even how to fit a kitchen.

Before you set yourself the challenge of trying a new skill, take some time to research. Read books, watch YouTube videos, and ask friends and family with experience for their help.

There are limits to what we would do. Neither Mr Shoestring nor I would mess with plumbing or electrics, for example, and prefer to leave such jobs to the professionals.

However, it is worth considering whether you could learn how to do a particular task yourself before you pay a large sum of money to a tradesman. The more you try, the more your confidence will grow.

Buy second-hand

As I mentioned in *Chapter 5*, second-hand is our default position when it comes to furniture. Over the years, this has saved us thousands of pounds.

You really can buy anything second-hand. We have recently begun looking for a second-hand kitchen. They often come up on Facebook Marketplace. We will have to refit it to suit our kitchen layout but buying second-hand could mean spending £500 rather than £5000 plus!

Alternatively, you could forget about a fitted kitchen altogether and pull a range of pre-loved free-standing cupboards, open shelving and dressers together instead. If you don't like the mismatched look, you could paint them all the same colour.

Reclamation yards can be good places to search for the elements to make up your free-standing kitchen. Charity shops such as Emmaus and the British Heart Foundation sometimes have furniture outlets too, which are full of pre-loved bargains in good condition. They deliver locally for a small fee.

Upcycling

I belong to a couple of Facebook groups where people share their upcycled pieces of furniture, and am constantly stunned by the budget transformations achieved.

With some decent paint, new knobs or handles, reupholstering, etc. you can make an old item look better than new. You can get even more creative with decoupage, stencils or by adding some gold leaf for a luxe look.

The web is awash with ideas for upcycling projects to give you some ideas and inspiration.

Getting materials for free

If your budget is really tight, it is possible to pick up items for your frugal home for free.

You can obtain part-used cans of paint by checking to see if you have a Community Repaint scheme in your area. If you don't, why not start one? Scrap stores exist in some towns and can be a great resource. They are often intended to provide craft supplies to children's organisations, but can be a good source of DIY materials too. Do an internet search to find your nearest.

Freecycle or Freegle can be excellent places to request paint and other DIY materials for free. People frequently have sheds full of part-used products that they will be pleased to get rid of.

We have found open but almost full cans of paint, items of furniture, crockery, curtains, rugs and more for free outside neighbour's houses. They are happy for you to take them away to stop them being wasted and to save them a trip to the tip.

Speaking of which, some local authorities and charities now run 'tip shops', where items saved from landfill are sold off very cheaply. These are an absolute treasure trove for the bargain hunter.

As I said in Chapter 5, skips can also be a brilliant source of DIY materials. Remember to ask permission before taking anything out, though.

Sewing, knitting and crochet

Like DIY skills, learning crafts such as sewing, knitting, quilting and crochet are not only fun hobbies. They can save you a lot of money when you are putting together your frugal home.

At its most basic, being able to alter a pair of curtains to fit a different room can give an old pair a new lease of life. Curtains, blinds, lampshades, throws and cushion covers can be created from fabrics purchased cheaply in charity shops and thrift stores.

Another member of my Facebook group, Yvonne, makes stunning quilts entirely from scrap fabrics. These beautiful pieces will be the antiques of the future and are completely unique.

Knitting and crochet have recently had an upsurge in popularity. Although wool can be quite pricey to buy, it is possible to follow our grandmothers' example and unravel existing woollen garments to reuse the wool. Knitting on the Net gives detailed instructions on how to do this.

People also frequently have half-finished wool projects and unused wool sitting in their cupboards. A request on Freegle or Freecycle could produce some free materials for your future knitting and crochet tasks.

If you have ever seen an outdoor crochet yarn bombing, you will know how much fun and colour crochet can bring. Bright crochet cushions and throws can create a homely, shabby chic feel that defies fashion.

Buy cheap, buy twice?

We all love a bargain. But when you are looking for new items for your home, it is easy to be seduced by cheap prices at the expense of quality.

Our grandparents didn't have the option to purchase cheap, mass-produced items. As it wouldn't occur to them to change their furniture and decor every few years, they bought things to last.

It could actually save money (as well as protecting our fragile environment) if we followed their example. Buying the best quality that you can possibly afford may involve saving up initially, but hopefully you will have an item that will last for many years.

This is one of the reasons that I look out for solid, vintage pieces of wooden furniture. They have lasted this long because they were made to. If you don't like the style or colour, you can always upcycle them! Consider buying once and buying well when you are creating your frugal home.

Chapter 8: The Frugal Cleaner

"Excuse the mess, but we live here." - Roseanne Barr

The manufacture of cleaning products is big business. Indeed, you can buy separate cleaners for your kitchen sink, oven, work surfaces, flooring, bathroom, shower and furniture.

You 'need' a specialist glass and tile spray and a carpet freshener as well, plus don't forget the different cloths, mops and brushes for each job. If you can't be bothered to wash your cleaning cloths between jobs, you can purchase disposable wipes instead.

The advertisers suggest that if only we would buy x, y or z product our homes could look as perfect and clean as Mrs Hinch's. We can make everything shine and the air will be as fresh as a meadow. Our clothing will be as soft as a baby's cheeks. Stains will melt away and our whites will be 'whiter than white'

We seem to be obsessed with killing germs. This is sometimes useful, like when someone in the house has a bout of winter vomiting virus or the dreaded Covid and you want to try to curb its spread with some serious disinfecting.

However, day to day, I don't believe we need to kill every tiny organism we live with. Some of them are actually beneficial to our health and we do have an immune system for a reason.

It's no wonder that most households have cupboards crammed full of cleaning items. These can add up to quite an expense, but how many of them are actually essential?

GREAT-GRANDMA'S CLEANING PRODUCTS

Think about your great-grandma's cleaning products (and, yes, it would have been her doing all the cleaning!). She would have had cloth and feather dusters, along with carbolic soap, which would have cleaned dishes, laundry and people too. Rags would have been used to wipe things down and wire wool to scrub stubborn pots. Hot water, washing soda, a good scrubbing brush and plenty of elbow grease would have been pretty much all that was needed in the early 20th century.

By the 1950s, manufacturers had started to make things a little easier for the housewife, with the introduction of scouring powders such as Ajax and washing up liquid. However, hard linoleum floors were still often cleaned with a cup of vinegar in hot water.

If the human race survived with such basic products for so long, then there is probably no reason why we couldn't dramatically reduce the number of cleaners in our cupboards with no ill effects. Not only would this save us money, it would reduce the chemical load in our homes.

MODERN BUT MINIMALIST CLEANING

Often, the simplest products are the cheapest and the least damaging.

Essential products for the frugal cleaner are white vinegar, soda crystals (aka washing soda), citric acid, baking soda and, maybe, some supermarket own brand bleach. You might add beeswax polish, borax substitute, essential oils and some castile soap (in either liquid or solid form).

Here are some suggestions to save money on cleaning whilst reducing the chemicals in your home in the process.

Cloths and wipes

Disposable wipes that clean and disinfect your surfaces, floors and bathroom can cost a pretty penny, are incredibly wasteful and have a detrimental effect on the environment.

They often contain plastic and are not biodegradable. Many are flushed down toilets and end up causing blockages in our sewage system. Even worse, in 2016 the Guardian reported that in the UK there had been "a 400% increase in the quantity of wet wipes found along our coastline over the past decade."

I find them much more difficult to use than fabric cloths, which are sturdier and can be rinsed out as you go. Similarly, floor mops with disposable wipes have to be changed frequently and are fiddly to use.

Instead, cut up a worn-out t-shirt or towel for cleaning, and invest in an old-fashioned mop and bucket. If you don't fancy that, a good steam mop can be an effective alternative.

Steel wool is great for tough cleaning jobs, and can be put in the metal recycling when it starts falling apart.

Soak your cleaning cloths in a little bleach, vinegar or disinfectant between uses, or wash them with your laundry.

Paper kitchen towels

Similarly, squares cut from old towels are great for all the jobs you would usually use paper kitchen rolls for. Mopping up spills, cleaning surfaces - even blowing your nose!

I no longer buy kitchen rolls. Instead, I keep an attractive basket full of towelling squares in the kitchen and throw them straight into the washing machine after use.

Laundry

Laundry powder in a cardboard box is cheaper and more eco-friendly than washing liquid, which comes in plastic bottles. I generally use half the recommended dose.

As an alternative to commercial laundry soap, you could try an Ecoegg, a reusable plastic 'egg' filled with mineral pellets. According to the manufacturers, the pellets contain biodegradable surfactants, which lift dirt from the fabrics being washed.

Soap nuts are another possibility for frugal, chemical free clothes cleaning. Soap nuts are dried soap berries, which contain a natural soap called saponin. They are cheap to buy and completely biodegradable.

Conkers also contain saponin and can be used for your laundry. There are various YouTube videos showing you how to prepare them.

You can, of course, make your own laundry detergent. The internet offers a wealth of recipes. In her book *Natural Household Cleaning*, Rachelle Strauss suggests making laundry 'gloop' by dissolving 140g/ 5oz of castile soap in four litres/seven pints of boiling water, before stirring in 125g/4.5oz of soda crystals. You use half a tea cup per laundry load.

Fabric softener

I have stopped using fabric softener altogether. I find a quarter of a cup of white vinegar (about 60 ml/two fl oz) works just as well and is much cheaper.

Citric acid is another option. Dissolve 20g/3/4 oz in 500ml/1 pint of water and use exactly as you would fabric softener.

Both have the added bonus of helping to keep your machine free of limescale.

In reality, most of the time I just don't bother. Domestic guru and author Shannon Lush actually recommends skipping the fabric softener as "it will damage your clothes, it is basically oil".

Washing up liquid

I always dilute our washing up liquid. In the first place, I only buy the cheap stuff from Aldi or

Lidl. You still use the same size squirt, it washes the dishes perfectly well and lasts twice as long.

A more eco-friendly alternative for dishwashing is a solid bar of castile soap. Get yourself a natural bristle brush, load it up with soap and it will leave your dishes sparkly clean without the plastic.

As mentioned previously, reusable dishcloths are more economical than the disposable variety.

Dishwashers

If you use a dishwasher, you could consider making your own powder. Most recipes are based on washing soda and easily found with an internet search.

Pure white vinegar can be used in place of rinse aid, and will keep your dishwasher clean too.

If you prefer to buy commercial dishwasher tablets, avoid the well known brands in favour of the supermarket own ones, which are much cheaper. As a bonus, many are now plastic free these days.

Ovens

I am not a fan of commercial oven cleaners. The harsh chemicals they contain stink the house out, make me feel wheezy and the smell lingers each time you put the oven on.

I have found soda crystals and some steel wool to be highly effective (better, in fact, than the commercial cleaners I used in the past). Simply sprinkle them on the bottom of the oven, add a small amount of hot water, leave for 20 minutes or so and start scrubbing! I recommend that you wear rubber gloves for this task.

Rinse well to avoid any residue.

Hobs and sinks

A solution of soda crystals dissolved in hot water will also clean your hob and your sink. Use about 250g/9 oz to 500 ml/1 pint of water. However, please note that soda crystals are not suitable for cleaning aluminium hobs.

If you have hard water and want to remove limescale from your sink, dip a damp cloth into a pot of citric acid and scrub it away.

Kitchen surfaces

I find a 50-50 mix of white vinegar and water perfect for cleaning and disinfecting work surfaces and chopping boards in the kitchen.

If you aren't keen on a strong vinegar smell, it is very easy to make a cleaner using citrus peels, such as my homemade all-purpose cleaning spray recipe below. This still uses vinegar, but the smell is diluted. Either way, I find that the vinegar aroma soon dissipates.

HOMEMADE ALL-PURPOSE CLEANING SPRAY

You will need:

The rinds of two or more lemons (I save them after baking)
Around half a litre/1 pint of white vinegar
A suitable glass container with lid
An old spray bottle

Method:

Add the lemon rinds to the glass container. Pour over the vinegar and put the lid on. Leave for two weeks. Strain into a large measuring jug. Check how much vinegar you have and then add the same amount of cold water. Give it a stir then pour into your spray container.

Floor cleaners

For a quick clean of a hard floor, your 50-50 vinegar spray wiped over with a damp mop is very effective.

If your floors need a good wash, a squirt of washing up liquid, liquid castile soap or soda crystals mixed in a bucket of hot water will do the trick.

Windows and mirrors

Internal glass can be cleaned with a 50-50 white vinegar and water spray.

If you want to wash the outside of your windows, try the old-fashioned method favoured by your grandmother. Fill a bucket with half hot water and half white vinegar, clean each pane with a sponge or cloth and dry to streak free perfection with scrunched up newspaper. You might find a lint free cloth useful for glass and window cleaning too.

Bathroom cleaning

I use my homemade lemon cleaner for a quick blitz of the bathroom. However, I find that for a thorough clean of greasy areas a little more cleaning power is required.

Baking soda sprinkled into the bath makes a good, eco-friendly scouring powder. Alternatively, Dri-Pak now sells Bicarb Cream, a gently abrasive, general-purpose cleaner that is ideal for sinks, baths and toilets.

WHY SHOULD WE WORRY ABOUT CHEMICALS?

We live in a toxic world. According to an article in *The Guardian* in May 2019, "Synthetic chemicals are in nearly everything we touch and consume. But some chemicals can be potentially harmful and a number of experts are anxious about possible long-term health effects of our everyday exposure." Sounds terrifying!

Although the chemicals in cleaners, personal care products, our food and even our furniture may have been tested individually, no one has tested their possible hazards to our health when they are mixed together.

The great thing about following a simpler, more natural and frugal cleaning routine is that you will easily reduce the chemical load in your home, as well as saving money. With this in mind, here are some products that you could cut from your shopping list to create a healthier environment in your home and spend less.

TOXIC HOUSEHOLD PRODUCTS YOU DON'T NEED

1 Laundry scent boosters

I was amazed the first time I encountered a bottle of bead-like perfumed balls on sale. Surely, with most washing detergents containing scent as well as fabric softeners, this is a totally pointless product?

If you really want your clothes and bedding to have a strong, pleasant smell, try spraying them with water infused with essential oils as they are drying or before you iron them.

2 Dryer sheets

I remember when tumble dryers existed but dryer sheets didn't. So why are they on offer? Why do we 'need' them? Like laundry scent boosters, they add yet more artificial perfume to our washing, along with other chemicals that, according to Eco Watch, "rub off the dryer sheet and coat your clothing in a slimy layer that has the effect of making your clothes feel softer."

When you put it like that, they don't sound so attractive, and when you consider that the chemicals in dryer sheets can cause some serious health problems like breathing difficulties, headaches and dizziness, you might want to give them a miss.

Eco Watch suggests using wool dryer balls instead, as they: "...don't contain toxic chemicals, they last for thousands of loads, get rid of static and wrinkles, soften clothes, and they actually save time and energy by cutting down on drying time."

3 In cistern 'blue' loo cleaners

The blue tablets that you place inside the cistern or hang from the toilet bowl are completely unnecessary. Your loo really doesn't need a load of chemicals blasted down it every time you flush.

In fact, according to an article on the *Today* website, entitled *10 Things Your Plumber Wishes You Wouldn't Do*, the chemicals in these products can even damage your toilet over time. If you are really paranoid that germs will take over in between cleans, try putting a cup of white vinegar in the pan every now and again.

4 Spray furniture polish

Spray polish may leave your furniture shiny, but if you look at the warnings on the cans you might think twice about using them in your home. They often contain phenol, which can cause headaches, dizziness and can even be fatal in rare circumstances.

According to Rachelle Strauss, nitrobenzene is another common ingredient that should be avoided. It "... is highly toxic, readily absorbed through the skin, and can cause severe damage to the central nervous system..."

Instead, a 50-50 mix of white vinegar and water in a spray bottle, as mentioned above, will clean most surfaces perfectly. If you want to add a shine to your wood, invest in a tin of proper beeswax polish. You only need to rub in a little and then buff it up.

5 Ironing water

Ironing water - the scented, distilled water that you put in your iron - is yet another product that never existed when I first bought an iron (showing my age again!).

Manufacturers claim that it prevents limescale development in your iron, makes ironing clothes easier and leaves them smelling like a meadow. However, *Which?* has suggested that ironing water is a totally unnecessary product that might actually damage your iron.

They spoke to Tefal, who apparently said, "Scented or treated waters can damage your iron or generator, as the chemicals leave residue which can damage seals and moving parts. Treated water can also have a higher boiling point, which can result in incomplete steam generation."

I have found that using boiled, cooled water with a few drops of essential oil is just as good, but you could equally well use water from your tap.

A WORD ABOUT BAKING SODA

Another cheap and effective must-have product in your frugal cleaning kit is something you probably have in your kitchen cupboard already - baking soda. Also known as bicarbonate of soda or baking powder, it is not to be confused with soda crystals. Baking soda is edible and is often used as a raising agent in baked goods. However, soda crystals are caustic and are definitely not to be eaten!

Baking soda can be used in many of the same ways as soda crystals, but are gentler and have excellent deodorising properties.

Have you ever walked into your kitchen on a hot day to the smell of nasty stuff fermenting in your bin? When this happens, I immediately reach for the bicarbonate of soda. If I remember to sprinkle some of this magical powder into the bins before I put in new liners, they don't get so smelly.

We always keep a big tub of baking soda handy. It is incredibly cheap for something that is so versatile.

I use wood pellets in the cat litter tray, as it is better at absorbing smells, but I also sprinkle baking soda at the bottom of the tray to keep the cat wee smell at bay for longer.

Bicarbonate of soda is good for getting rid of nasty odours in the fridge too; just leave a small bowlful at the bottom and it will help neutralise the smell.

Use it as a scouring powder on dirt and stains pretty much anywhere in the house. Sprinkle it on a damp sponge and give surfaces a good scrub - it isn't harsh so won't scratch them. Tip it down the plug hole with half a cup of white vinegar to alleviate smelly drains then use it to scrub the sink.

You can mix it to a paste with some water to remove mould around windows, walls and ceilings.

Pans and dishes with stubborn stains and dried-on food can be soaked in a bowl with a couple of tablespoons of bicarbonate of soda before hand washing or placing in your dishwasher. This also works on tea-stained mugs.

Sprinkle baking soda onto smelly sofas, rugs or carpets, leave for half an hour or so then vacuum. It is especially good at getting rid of pet smells.

If you have heavily soiled laundry, try adding half a cup of soda alongside your washing powder or liquid. It will also brighten light-coloured items.

When the natural, old-fashioned approach to cleaning can save you lots of money too, it is worth investigating.

Chapter 9: The Frugal Garden

"The glory of gardening: hands in the dirt, head in the sun, heart with nature. To nurture a garden is to feed not just the body, but the soul." – **Alfred Austin**

I come from a long line of gardeners. As a child, I remember visiting my old grandad. Even though he only had a little garden at the back of his council house, he managed to squeeze in a greenhouse and small vegetable patch, and always grew some food.

Lettuces, tomatoes, cucumbers, a few runner beans, peas and some cabbages were standard.

Later, my dad followed suit, turning the bottom of our garden into a big allotment. He added to his own father's repertoire with carrots, broccoli, onions, potatoes, courgettes, broad beans and more.

He also made the rest of the garden beautiful, and it was always rammed full of his homegrown flowers and shrubs.

Not that I took much interest. As a teenager, I thought nothing was more boring than gardening and wasn't at all impressed by my dad's green-fingered prowess.

Once I hit my forties, my genes kicked in. I am in no way an expert gardener, but you don't really have to be. We enjoy growing and eating our own homegrown fruit and vegetables, and like to fill the garden with flowers.

I have discovered that, however amateur a gardener you are, seeds want to grow! They just need a bit of soil, some sunshine and water and they are away.

Even better, you really don't need to spend a fortune on your garden, although it is very easy to do so. If you let me loose in a garden centre with a couple of hundred pounds, I would happily spend it. However, there are lots of ways to create a beautiful and productive garden on a budget.

BUDGET GARDENING TIPS

Digging for victory…

During the second world war, the UK population was encouraged to 'dig for victory'. Every bit of garden and common land was cultivated to make sure people were fed, as it became too risky and precarious to rely on imports.

If you have a little bit of garden, you could grow a few tomatoes, courgettes, herbs and potatoes. Even if you only have a patio, it is possible to grow some of your own food.

It is incredibly cheap to turn a pack of seeds into food for your family. It will also have far fewer, if any, chemicals, no plastic packaging, no food miles and will, of course, save you money.

Grow your own plants from seed

This is the number one way to save money in the garden. I love nothing more than a mosey in a garden centre, but plants can be expensive! Growing your own plants from seed is so cheap. You can soon fill large spaces with beautiful flowers. If you choose varieties that self seed they will arrive year on year.

Take cuttings

Taking cuttings from established plants is another skill worth cultivating. We have a garden full of beautiful wallflowers because Mr Shoestring loves them and is always growing more this way.

Make compost

Making your own compost has so many benefits. A lot of wildlife loves a compost heap, it is an eco-friendly way to get rid of raw fruit and vegetable scraps from the kitchen, paper and cardboard, lawn clippings, etc and it creates wonderful nutrient rich material to feed your plants.

In addition, cash-strapped local councils are increasingly charging to take away garden waste. If you want to save money, it makes sense to compost.

You can create a compost box system out of old wood and pallets or buy a plastic composter. Local councils often have offers on these.

We have both: a plastic one for the tea leaves and kitchen scraps near the house and a couple of larger ones created from pallets for lawn clippings and other waste at the bottom of the garden.

When it comes to using compost, whether you make your own or buy it, you can save money by filling the bottom section of larger pots with broken pots and crockery. This helps drainage too.

If you have some trees in your garden or near to your home, you can also make leaf mould. It is a lovely soil conditioner and easy to make. For most of us, it is usually very easy to get hold of leaves in the autumn.

Throw your damp leaves into bin liners (moisten them if they are dry or they won't rot down), then make holes in the bag, tie the top loosely and stack the bags out of the way for a year or so.

Free manure

Keep an eye out for free horse manure. Individuals and riding stables are often happy to give it away just to get rid of it, so if you know somebody who owns a horse, ask them.

Tip: Keep an old sheet in your car boot to protect it from spillages. Even with this, be prepared for your car to smell a bit ripe! Don't use fresh manure on your garden immediately, as it needs to rot down for a year or so first.

Even better than horse manure, if you know somebody who keeps chickens, ask if you can take away their droppings when their run is cleaned out. Chicken droppings are high in nutrients and make a great free fertiliser.

Share seeds and plants

Most seed packets contain way more seeds than anyone would want to grow in one go. They do last for a few years even if opened. In fact, I germinated some flower seeds I found that were five years out of date. (This doesn't always work - some types will fail if they are too old.)

You can save money by sharing seed packets with friends and family (or on the allotment if you are lucky enough to have one) or do a seedling swap if you have grown too much of anything.

Grow crops that are expensive to buy

Whilst it is fun to grow onions and potatoes, they are cheap to buy anyway. Asparagus, on the other hand, isn't! Especially if you have little space, it can make sense to concentrate your efforts on crops that are expensive to purchase.

The staples are grown in our garden too, but you can save money on high value crops by growing them yourself.

One of my favourite vegetables to grow is the humble runner bean, which is still a strictly seasonal crop. Because they are only around for a few weeks in the summer, they can be quite expensive.

Courgettes are another popular one here because they freeze well. They are great for soup later in the year.

Plant a herb garden

Similarly, if you are a cook, it is easy to spend quite a lot on fresh herbs in the supermarket. Planting your own herb garden near the kitchen will give you a fresh supply all through the summer months, and you can freeze or dry some for winter.

If you don't want to grow lots of herbs from seed, try potting on plants purchased from the supermarket. This has worked well for us in the past.

Sell your extra plants and produce

We can't help but screech to a halt when we pass a little stall selling plants or homegrown fruit and vegetables outside people's houses. They are usually at a bargain price with an honesty box, which we always add to.

If you have excess produce of your own and live somewhere you will get passers-by, you can make a little extra cash selling them.

Don't buy pots

Don't get me wrong, I love a beautiful container. However, you really don't need to spend a lot of money on them. I like to recycle pots and containers, which is environmentally friendly as well as saving money in the garden.

You can use almost anything that you can make a drainage hole in as a place to grow plants. I keep my old wellies for this purpose, as they look lovely with some trailing flowers in them.

But don't stop at the small stuff - before you dump your old toilet, just think how good it might look planted up with summer flowers. Painted tyres can be piled up to make little raised beds too.

We keep various plastic food pots and containers for the garden. Trays from ready meals, which are frequently unrecyclable, work perfectly well as seed trays, along with mushroom containers, grape pots, etc. Yoghurt pots are good for potting your seeds on and also for cutting up to use as plant labels.

Old terracotta pots can be given a new lease of life with a coat of paint. Who hasn't got a shed full of half-full paint tins?

Buy second-hand tools

Decent quality garden tools, such as forks, spades, trowels, etc can cost a pretty penny when purchased new. However, we often manage to pick up second-hand garden implements when we go to boot sales in the summer. If they have been used and still look good, they were probably good quality in the first place and will hopefully last a few more years.

You can also find various garden paraphernalia on Facebook selling groups, or you can put a wanted request at your local Freecycle or Freegle group.

However, if you are buying garden implements from new, buy the best quality you can afford so that they will last for many years.

Install water butts and conserve water

It is really important to install water butts in your garden if you want to save money, particularly if you are on a water meter. In the summer, when it is hot and dry and your plants are thirsty, using the supplies in the water butts first will save you loads. In addition, a lot of plants actually prefer rain water.

As our climate warms, water will become an increasingly precious resource, so a couple of water butts in the garden is good for the environment too.

Unless you have a massive garden, water your plants with a watering can rather than a hose to reduce your usage. If you do use a hose, invest in a trigger nozzle to control the flow as you need it.

Similarly, if you want to save money and water, don't use a water sprinkler on your lawn. They can use up to 1000 litres of water an hour. Brown grass will not die and it will recover as soon as it rains.

Create a wildlife patch

How is creating a wildlife patch saving money in the garden, I hear you ask? There are many advantages to having a wildlife garden. Wild areas will attract more birds, insects, frogs and toads to eat some of the slugs and other pests that frequently visit, they cost very little to implement and they create an attractive area for you to watch nature.

We have a pile of old branches and twigs at the end of our garden where stag beetles hatch (and we eventually hope to find a hedgehog or some slow worms), areas of longer grass and wildflowers, and half a barrel filled with water in lieu of a pond. Of course, a larger pond will attract even more wildlife into your garden, but our half barrel will do for now.

A wildlife area saves time as well as money as it requires minimal intervention.

Upcycle

Before you rush to the garden centre to buy new garden furniture, can you improve what you already have? Or can you pick up something second-hand, even if it is a bit battered, and upcycle it? This is a great way to save money in the garden, as good furniture can be very expensive.

We still have a lovely bench we found outside a neighbour's house several years ago. It had no seat but the basic structure was sound and made from good quality wood. We walked it the short distance home, Mr Shoestring set about repairing it and I painted it a light green. It looked fabulous, and is still going strong.

The absolute best example of upcycling I have ever seen in the garden is from blogger Iona at Life After Money, who made a summerhouse almost completely from scrap. She used pallets, doors and timber collected from skips, and contacted a double-glazing company who said she could have some old windows that they had removed from their customers' homes.

Iona also got the roof panels for £20 from a conservatory company, which had a yard full of them.

She asked around for half full tins of old paint, mixing colours to suit herself and painting the summer house various bright shades.

Finally, she filled it with old painted furniture, made bunting, curtains and cushion covers and placed pot plants at the entrance. It looks amazing, and even featured on Channel 4's

Shed of the Year, winning the Budget Shed category!

Make do and mend

Mr Shoestring hates throwing something away if he can repair it. We are still using a wheelbarrow he pulled out of a ditch. It was very rusty, but he gave it a new sheet of metal on the bottom and it is fully functioning, if not exactly beautiful.

The trick is to think twice before you throw something away to see if there is any way to make it do or mend it.

Don't only buy plants from the garden centre

As I previously admitted, I love a leisurely peruse of the garden centre and would happily spend a small fortune if I could afford it. However, there are cheaper places to purchase plants.

The discount supermarkets and retailers such as Home Bargains, B&M, Aldi and Lidl are all excellent for good value plants. However, you need to get them shortly after they arrive at these stores as they don't get looked after as well as they do in the specialist garden centres.

Summer fetes and festivals can be great for cheap plants as well, plus stalls outside people's homes.

Check out the reduced section

Yellow stickers aren't just for food! It is always worth heading for the discounted items at garden centres too.

Sometimes you can bring tired-looking plants back to life that you find there, particularly if they are shrubs or perennials.

Dealing with pests

You can spend a lot of money killing the pesky slugs found in every garden, not to mention the negative effects slug pellets can have on other wildlife. For a gentler solution, make slug traps using cheapest supermarket beer and old yoghurt or margarine pots.

For other pests, such as aphids and black fly, you can make an environment and budget friendly insecticidal soap spray, using two teaspoons of liquid castile soap to a litre of water.

If you are lucky enough to have some outside space, it makes sense to make the best of it. A lovely green area lifts the spirits, and gardening itself is an amazing way to get fit and keep the stress of the day job at bay.

Chapter 10: Frugal Fashion: Dress for Less

"I wear a lot of second-hand clothes, unless I have a concert and then I wear beaded and sequined second-hand clothes." - Chris Isaak

I'm no fashionista; I am happiest in my jeans and wellies. However, I do have three frugal style guru daughters, who know all the tricks to finding stylish bargains. They are the mistresses of frugal fashion!

We all refuse to spend a lot of money on clothes. Once you start finding frugal fashion bargains you resent paying full price for anything.

Here are our collective thoughts on frugal fashion.

Second-hand

The majority of my clothes are purchased second-hand. I find endless high-quality bargains at boot sales and rarely spend more than £1 or £2 per item. Some are actually new with tags; impulse purchases never worn by the previous owner.

I have come across lovely items that were originally very expensive from brands such as Monsoon, Phase Eight and Karen Millen, as well as good high street names such as Next, Marks and Spencer and the (now sadly departed) Laura Ashley.

However, as boot sales usually only run over the summer, charity shops are worth investigating too. You need to be prepared to spend more, obviously. I find some of them over-priced these days, but still cheaper than purchasing new items.

Happily, jumble sales appear to be making something of a comeback. Scout and Guide groups often run them as fund-raisers. Clothing is the cheapest of all at a jumble - sometimes as little as 10 or 20 pence per item. Garage sale trails are also more prevalent in the UK now.

Online pre-owned frugal fashion

Most people are aware of eBay as the place to 'bag a bargain', but Depop and Vinted are on the up and worth keeping an eye on.

My youngest daughter often looks for a particular item that she has seen at full price in the shops. She says they frequently pop up within just a few months of being bought and she can get them at a fraction of the original price.

The same daughter also makes a mental note of clothes that she loves at her favourite stores and makes a beeline for them in the sales. She often finds them at their sale prices. Patience really is a virtue!

Factory shops

Most towns have a factory shop somewhere that sells all kinds of things at great prices, including clothes and shoes. They are worth a look. Our local one would definitely attract an older clientele though.

Use cashback sites

If you need a dress or pair of shoes and just cannot wait for a sale, at least use a cashback site to see if the retailer is on there.

In fact, don't restrict cashback sites just to clothing. I use them for all of my online shopping. My favourites are TopCashback and Quidco.

Scaling down

Even those of us who consider ourselves frugal often have way too many clothes.

I am guilty of buying too many fantastic second-hand items, then ramming them in my cupboards and forgetting about them. My solution is a regular wardrobe declutter so that I circulate and wear each item to get good value out of it.

I am certainly not a minimalist, but I do like the idea of creating a capsule wardrobe. The idea is to own a small number of clothes in neutral colours that can be mixed and matched to make many different looks.

Men seem to do this less consciously, wearing standard suits, shirts and ties to work and for more formal occasions.

Certainly, our recent ancestors wouldn't have had cupboards full of clothing. They had their day-to-day work clothes and their Sunday best.

Look after your stuff

Because clothing is so cheap and easy to come by these days, we often don't value or look after our things in the same way that our grandparents would have.

However, if you really want to save money and make your clothing last, a few minutes spent taking care of it can pay dividends.

Shake out and hang up your clothes after wearing them. If they aren't dirty don't wash them, as this wears them out more quickly. Unless you do manual work, your clothing probably doesn't need laundering after just one wear. This is unlikely to apply to your messy children, though.

Items that aren't worn often are best stored under plastic covers, which can be purchased quite cheaply online.

When you have favourite pieces of clothing that are a little faded, a pack of coloured dye - the sort that you can put in your washing machine - can add new life to old garments.

This is also a good tip for towels, especially if you have an assortment of colours and want them all to match.

Look after your shoes. When I was a child, my parents often got our shoes resoled and reheeled. Nowadays, this is only financially worthwhile with expensive, high-quality footwear.

Nevertheless, I remember my dad's habit of cleaning our school shoes last thing on a Sunday evening ready for the new week. Buying decent leather footwear and looking after it in this way will make it last much longer.

Invest in a debobbler for your woollens and coats. This is a handy little gadget for those of us who prefer second-hand clothing.

Make do and mend

On the same theme, when you are aiming for old-fashioned frugality, learning to repair clothing is a worthwhile skill to nurture (see Chapter 4 for more on making do and mending).

It may seem a faff to sew up a hole in a sock, but that's the point of this book. It really only takes a couple of minutes - less time than buying a new pair.

Stain removal

Bicarbonate of soda or soda crystals are good for pre-soaking stained fabrics.

You can also soak in a 50/50 mix of water and white vinegar. This is particularly good for sweat odours and stains.

You can purchase commercial stain removers, of course, if you don't have the time or inclination to make your own. I prefer the solid bar type ones that you roll on and leave for a while before laundering.

Making your own clothes

In these days of fast fashion, making your clothing from scratch isn't necessarily cheaper. However, if you choose to do so it makes financial sense to use the fabric from current garments or upcycle them.

Just as our WW2 grandmothers did, old woollen garments can be unravelled and knitted into new items.

The Penny Pinchers Book, a classic from the 1990s by John and Irma Mustoe, suggests that when your old favourite items of clothing disintegrate you pick them apart and use them to make a pattern for a new garment.

Swap clothes

Children's clothing can be swapped between families, or handed down. Apps such as Vinted allow clothes to be swapped as well as sold.

Paying for the name

Designer clothing vs high street or supermarket own brands… are they really worth the extra expense or are you paying for the name?

Sometimes you can tell that a designer item is really great quality, but buying high end items second-hand, as I often do, I have found that is often not the case.

A pair of designer trainers costing £120 may be much better quality than a cheap plastic pair costing you a tenner, but are they really three times as good as a pair from a decent high street retailer costing £40? I think not. Of course, if you scour eBay and the charity shops you might find that designer pair lightly used for £20!

Buy clothing out of season

If you prefer to purchase something new, then it makes a lot of sense to buy in the sales. This may mean buying your winter coats in the spring and your summer apparel as you move into Autumn, but it will save you a lot of money if you do.

Think ahead to upcoming occasions, such as parties and weddings. The best time to buy a prom dress, for example, is just after Christmas, when the party gear has been reduced.

Buy children's clothing a size or two larger when you are buying ahead in this way.

Tights

Purchase thick, opaque tights rather than the fine 10 or 15 denier variety, as they last much longer.

It is said that if you put tights in the freezer overnight before you wear them they are slower to develop holes. You need to remove them from their packaging and run them under the tap, freeze overnight, thaw and dry them, and you are good to go.

Hand wash rather than machine wash tights and dry naturally rather than in the tumble dryer.

As soon as you see the start of a run on your tights, paint a little clear nail varnish on. An old trick, but it works!

Best bargain sites

Many good, expensive clothing brands have outlets, either on eBay or their own websites. For example, Joules has an eBay outlet store.

The clothing is often a third of the original retail price.

There are also websites such as Everything5Pounds, which sells ex-high street brands for, well, £5!

Chapter 11: Frugal Fun and Travel

"We're so busy watching out for what's just ahead of us that we don't take time to enjoy where we are." — Bill Watterson

Please don't confuse being frugal with being miserable. It doesn't mean you don't get to have fun! Indeed, adopting a generally frugal attitude can enable you to spend any spare cash on entertainment and experiences that more deeply enrich your life.

I think it is important to leave room in your budget for fun. What that looks like depends on what you and your family enjoy. It might be important to you to have a weekly takeaway or a meal out with your family; or perhaps you go to the cinema once a fortnight or to the pub.

Have a column in your budget for entertainment so that you only spend what you can comfortably afford.

Making conscious choices with your money might mean that you don't do everything you used to, or accept every invitation out with friends, but what you choose to do has the most value and meaning for you.

However, I have found that when you embrace a frugal lifestyle, you soon realise that there are many opportunities for fun and entertainment that are either extremely cheap or cost nothing at all.

Here are some ideas for frugal fun and travel.

CHEAPER MEALS OUT

One of the best ways to get a first-class restaurant experience at a massively reduced price is to find some student chefs to cook for you. We are lucky to have a college of further education that runs a catering and hospitality course. To give their students valuable experience, they run a real-life restaurant, staffed by the students but supervised by the tutors.

You can have a fine dining three-course lunch with coffee for £15, which is a huge treat for people on a budget. Check to see where your nearest catering school is.

Another way to get everything cheaper when eating out is to sign up as a mystery shopper. You usually (but not always - check the small print!) get the full cost of your meal refunded.

Sign up to as many mystery shopping sites as possible to get the most opportunities to eat out for free. You will have to follow specific instructions, like ordering a certain type of meal, so make sure you read them thoroughly.

Another way to have a cheap meal out is to see if you have a Real Junk Food Project Cafe in your area. This is an ingenious scheme using surplus food that would otherwise go to waste. The cafes are run by volunteers on a 'pay as you feel' basis. They are great for people with little money, although anyone can use them.

The movement's manifesto statement is 'feed bellies, not bins'.

To locate a pay as you feel cafe near you, it is best to do an internet search as locations and availability are subject to change. At the time of writing, the following cafes were operational:

Second Helpings Cafe, Stamford Methodist Church Hall, Barn Hill, Stamford, Lincolnshire PE9 3AE.

The Real Junk Food Project in Brighton runs cafes at several locations and has a website with details.

PAYF Cafe, LS-TEN, Unit 1 Kitson Road, Leeds LS10 1NT.

The West End PAYF Cafe, Andrewes Street, The West End Neighbourhood Centre, Leicester LE3 5PA.

FRUGAL DAYS OUT

Our best days out generally involve the cost of our transport and a picnic. We are blessed with some fabulous seaside towns and coastal paths nearby, as well as woodland walks and historic landmarks.

A typical Sunday will find us out for a hike with the dog, a flask and some sandwiches. Taking our own picnic dramatically reduces the cost of each outing.

We have discovered new and interesting walks practically on our doorstep using a free app called AllTrails.

You can search walks by area, length, difficulty and elevation, and even request certain types of landmarks, such as forests or historic sites.

Walking has the added advantage of being great, free exercise!

If you are a cyclist, you can use the app to locate suitable mountain bike friendly trails too.

However, please note that if you want access to the offline features of the AllTrails app, there is a charge.

Find free events

There are always a multitude of free community events on at any one time, such as talks, fairs and festivals, garage and yard sale trails, craft markets, yarn bombing, art shows and more. The skill is in finding them!

Keep an eye out for events advertised on community, school and church notice boards, in shop windows, as well as on your parish, town and county council websites. Look in your nearest tourist office for leaflets as well as your library. Check for open events at local colleges or universities too.

Facebook is also a good way to find out what free events are happening near you.

Open gardens

In the UK, there are often open garden events to visit for a small donation in the summer. These are either individual householders, stately homes or whole villages and towns who open their gardens up to raise money for a charity or community project.

It is lovely to have a nose around someone else's beautifully kept garden, have a chat with the gardener and pick up ideas for your own backyard. They often have tea and cake on offer too.

You can find a list of open garden events at opengardens.co.uk or the National Open Gardens Scheme (ngs.org.uk).

Events for seniors

For older people, it is worth checking the Age UK website, as they run a range of activities for seniors, such as arts and crafts, coffee mornings, lunch clubs and quizzes.

Another gem for older people is u3a, formerly the University of the Third Age, which offers a great range of free events and activities to members. There is a small membership fee of around £15.

u3a is described as "a UK wide, cooperative movement of people no longer in full time work who come together to continue their educational, social and creative interests in a friendly and informal environment."

From lectures, to gardening groups and exercise sessions, u3a members have a good choice of activities delivered by members to members.

Visit your local Wildlife Trust nature reserve

Joining and visiting a Wildlife Trust is a superb way to get out into nature, as well as supporting the preservation of wild spaces. The Wildlife

Trusts offer the chance for the children to run around and let off steam as well as for you and your family to learn about the wildlife in your area.

The Trusts are a campaigning organisation and have huge influence. You can join for just a few pounds each month, then visit for free.

Delve into a museum

In the UK, entry to our national museums is currently free. They are a fabulous way to teach your family about art and history.

One of our favourites is the Natural History Museum in London, but there are lots of smaller local museums that may be free too.

Have a look on your council website or on the Visit Britain website.

Making use of your local library

Settling down with a good book has always been a frugal form of entertainment, even more so if you borrow your books for free from the library.

However, many people don't realise that modern libraries offer ebooks and audiobooks too, as well as online journals and magazines that might cost you £5 a throw in paper form.

In fact, libraries are more than just a place to find books. You can use a computer for free, do online courses, take your toddlers to story time sessions or visit an exhibition.

Some larger libraries even offer sessions for job seekers, author events, book groups and basic computer courses.

Larger libraries often have a cafe and most have comfortable seating areas, where you can read newspapers and magazines for nothing.

Fun with friends on a budget

It can be hard on friendships when you adopt a more frugal lifestyle. Some people will assume you are cheap; others will lose interest when you can't keep up with their more affluent lifestyles.

You might be embarrassed to tell people that you have debts or are struggling financially. I don't see why you have to. They live their lives and you live yours. They can make their own financial decisions and shouldn't influence how you choose to live. Don't be ashamed because you are taking control of your finances and tackling your debts. This is something to be proud of!

I have found that the friends who really matter tend to stick around. On top of that, I have made new ones who have made a decision, like me, to live more frugally and sustainably.

That said, it is quite possible to have fun with your friends without spending a lot of money. Rather than going out to dinner or the pub, invite them to your house for a potluck dinner, where they each bring a dish and a bottle.

You could suggest meeting up for a walk and a picnic, visit a free museum, or have a games night. Just make sure that if you choose poker, you use matchsticks instead of money!

Search for discount vouchers

When you are planning a big day out or a visit to a concert, theatre or cinema, it is always worth checking cashback sites such as TopCashBack and Quidco for deals.

In addition, you can often find discounts and two-for-one offers for theme parks and other attractions on product packaging like cereal boxes and confectionery.

If you are a UK Tesco customer, Clubcard vouchers offer good value when you spend your accumulated points on days out.

CHEAP CHILDREN'S ACTIVITIES

Keeping children occupied, particularly during school vacations, can be an expensive business. That's why the subject deserves its own section. Here are eight ideas for children's activities that are either free or very low cost.

Leaf printing

Leaf printing is a lovely old-fashioned activity. Leaves are easy to find wherever you live. It is really two cheap children's activities in one as you will need a fun walk in the fresh air to collect the leaves first!

Choose plenty of different shapes of leaf and don't pick up the brittle ones as they will crumble too quickly.

Paint is cheap too, especially if you buy the powdered stuff and mix it yourself. Simply paint the leaves in different colours and press them onto card or paper. Very simple and effective.

Pond dipping

I loved going pond dipping with my kids when they were young. Obviously, you need to pay attention when you mix kids with water, so they must be closely supervised.

All you need is water – your own or a neighbour's pond is a good starting point – a sieve, a jam jar and a large light-coloured tray. There are some very good instructions for pond dipping on the Freshwater Habitats Trust website.

Recycled crafts

Save toilet roll tubes, sweet wrappers, bits of wool, wrapping paper, foil, fabric, etc and make a craft box. Invest in some PVA glue, some paint, pipe cleaners and any other craft supplies you find at reasonable prices.

On a cold, wet day your craft box will come into its own, allowing your children to be messy and creative.

Geocaching

The modern-day treasure hunt, geocaching is hugely popular and very addictive. You used to have to purchase a GPS device to take part, but now there are apps available for your smart phone very cheaply. Some are even free. There is a great beginner's guide to geocaching on the Ordnance Survey website.

Beach combing

If you are lucky enough to live near to the sea or are having a beach holiday, beachcombing is so much fun. Finding little treasures such as shells, sea glass and pretty stones costs nothing and kids love it. They can explore the wildlife in the rock pools whilst you are there, and maybe create some crafts with their finds back at home.

Charity shopping/boot sales

I love a good root around a summer boot sale. You can buy pretty much anything at a fraction of the as-new price.

I used to give my daughters five pounds each and let them spend it as they wished. This was a pleasant way to wile away some time and their finds entertained them back at home too.

Charity shops aren't as cheap, but you are supporting a good cause, and they are still great places to find bargains. Both offer an inexpensive opportunity to teach your children about money and budgeting.

Buying second-hand is also good for the environment, as you extend the useful life of the items you buy and stop them going to landfill.

Have a cookery session

Children love to cook! There are so many reasons why you should teach yours this essential life skill.

At its most basic level, it is fun and will wile away an afternoon or two. However, it also gives you the opportunity to discuss where food comes from and slip in some information about good nutrition.

In addition, cooking from scratch is cheaper and healthier than buying packaged meals and allows you to avoid excess packaging.

You could let your kids plan a meal and buy the ingredients as part of your cooking session. This will help to prepare them for independence as they get older.

Plant something

You don't have to have a garden to grow things with children. Cress is so easy to grow on your windowsill, along with various herbs. You can also attempt to sprout avocado seeds or regrow lettuce.

Romaine works best, but you can try this with any lettuce. You need to cut the stem about two inches from the base and place it in a shallow dish with just enough water to cover the bottom section. Place it on a sunny windowsill and change the water every couple of days.

Eventually, the leaves will start to regrow. You won't get enough for a whole salad, but your kids can cut the leaves off to put in their sandwiches.

If you are fortunate enough to have a vegetable patch, involve your children and give them a bit of earth to grow a few bits in. They will get the same satisfaction from growing their own food as you do.

Having fun with your children doesn't always have to involve a huge amount of expense. With these ideas for cheap children's activities, you may find the most enduring memories you make are those that cost very little.

FRUGAL HOLIDAYS

Mr Shoestring and I work hard all year. We scrimp and save and live a frugal lifestyle to make sure bills are paid and no debts accrued. One thing we insist on, however, is at least one holiday a year. We don't spend a fortune; we don't need to as we know how to get the best value for our money.

Building it into our budget

Building a holiday fund into our budget is important to us. We don't run an expensive car, have lots of nights in the pub or wear designer clothing. Because of this, for the last few years we have managed two holidays every year. It depends what your priorities are and this is what we like to do. If you enjoy a getaway and you can afford it, try to save a regular amount towards this.

Look out of the box

Some of our best and cheapest holidays have been found because we don't mind our accommodation being basic and are more interested in our location.

Many years ago, I spotted a tiny ad in a magazine advertising a caravan on an organic smallholding in Wales. I contacted the owner, who emailed us some photographs of a 1970s caravan, complete with brown and orange decor of the era. It looked clean and comfortable with a small kitchen area and shower room, and most intriguing of all, it featured a compost toilet built on the side!

We took a chance on this eccentric little place, and had many happy holidays there, until the owners retired and sold up.

Another good find was a hilltop chalet park on the Norfolk coast. It had few facilities and the chalets were too tiny to appeal to most families. They couldn't be described as luxurious, but nevertheless the chalets were warm and comfortable and had the most stunning views of the sea.

It pays to be open minded about your potential holiday accommodation and look for something quirky that perhaps won't appeal to the masses.

Home swapping

Another way to get your holiday more cheaply is to do a home swap. The big advantage is that your (usually comfortable and well-equipped) accommodation is free. In addition, someone is looking after your home whilst you are away.

However, you do still need to get there. We drove to France and Spain for our home swaps. The latter was a long journey with relatively young children and we did need to stop over at a cheap hotel on the way, which obviously added to the cost. However, there is no reason you can't house swap in your own country, especially if you live somewhere generally popular with tourists.

A disadvantage of house swapping is the amount of work that goes into getting your place ready for visitors. You need everything to be very clean and tidy, and your house needs to be in good decorative order.

I suggest you use a house exchange organisation, but they do charge a fee. Shop around to get the best deal.

The Sun newspaper holidays

A couple of times a year *The Sun* newspaper runs a £9.50 holiday promotion. You collect ten tokens from the paper and can book a three or four-night holiday for four people for a starting price of £9.50. In reality, once you have added any extras charged by the individual parks, they generally cost more than this, but are still very good value and worth investigating.

You do have to be quick, however, as they get booked up extremely quickly. It's often not possible to get your first choice so you need to be prepared to be flexible on location.

WWOOFing

Fancy a working holiday on a farm? WWoofing (Worldwide Opportunities On Organic Farms) allows you to do just that.

If you are in good physical and mental health with a genuine interest in farming practices, you can volunteer to work on farms throughout the world in exchange for your bed and board. You do need to pay a subscription to the host country's WWOOF organisation and your own travel costs. However, this can be a great cultural experience and you are likely to make many friends from around the world.

Camping

Camping as a family is probably the cheapest holiday option of all. However, it can be expensive to buy all of the gear to start with. You will need a large tent, inflatable mattresses, sleeping bags, lights, a gas cooker, and utensils like a kettle, pots, pans, plates, cups, etc as a minimum. I would also go for a fold up table, a wind break and some comfy chairs.

If you are going to go away regularly you will soon recoup the costs. However, it is a good idea to try to borrow the gear to begin with to make sure you will be a happy camper.

If you are staying under canvas in the UK, you will all need a decent set of waterproofs. You are at the mercy of the weather. We had many fabulous camping holidays when the kids were young. However, If I am being honest, we also bailed on a couple. One because of continuous, heavy rain and the other because the winds were so bad our tent almost got blown away!

We bought our tent in the sale at the end of the summer and managed to pick up some other bits second-hand. We were even given some camping gear on Freecycle. Overall, camping is a great frugal holiday choice for families.

Hostels

Another good option for value accommodation is the Youth Hostels Association. Despite the name, they welcome holidaymakers of all ages.

When I was younger I found YHAs were always an excellent option for the tourist on a budget. In those days the accommodation was basic and you had to do some jobs in order to stay, such as clean the loos or sweep the stairs. It was fun and a great way of meeting your fellow travellers.

These days, the YHA offers a range of accommodation, from private rooms similar to hotels, to campsites and camping pods. However, they still have some more traditional dormitory hostel accommodation, which is by far your cheapest option, starting from around £13 per night.

The YHA isn't the only provider of hostel beds, although I know from speaking to some of the language students we have hosted that the quality of the accommodation isn't always great. Sometimes you are packed into rooms that aren't very clean and are sometimes they are mixed sex. Do some research before you book.

Become a house sitter

There are various house-sitting organisations that match house sitters with accommodation and offer opportunities all over the world. The premise is that you look after someone's house and pets for free and you get to stay in their home in return.

You have to pay your own travel costs, and obviously need to take your responsibility as a pet sitter seriously.

Airbnb

When we splash out on accommodation, we tend to use Airbnb. There is a range of property on offer. The cheapest we found was the spare bedroom of a young lady's house on Anglesey Island in Wales. It was extremely basic, but it did the job and was much cheaper than staying in a regular hotel or B&B.

You can rent out anything from a room in a family home for the night to a chalet in the garden or a whole city apartment.

Couchsurfing

A completely free way to stay in a new place is to join the Couchsurfing community. As the name suggests, you can stay on someone's couch, spare room or even an air mattress on the floor of the sitting room for free!

The Couchsurfing.com website offers you a way to connect and befriend fellow travellers around the globe. The organisation gives plenty of safety advice and encourages regular community meetups and events.

This is a great option for the adventurous student or singleton.

Other things to consider

If you are travelling as a family or group, renting self-catering accommodation will tend to be cheaper than booking a hotel. Couples, however, may be able to find cheaper hotel deals.

Food

Self-catering whilst you are away is generally the most economical way to eat. However, if you shop around for a cheap, all-inclusive deal you might come up trumps.

On a trip to Mallorca a few years ago, we found an all-in hotel deal that included accommodation for a week, all food and drink, plus airport transfers for £100 cheaper than the room only deal at the hotel next door.

If you do go for self-catering, packing a picnic most days with drinks and treats, especially when you have children with you, will save you a ton of money.

TRANSPORT

Car sharing

Car sharing organisations such as BlaBlaCar and Lift Share are worth exploring when you are planning a journey. They give you the option to share the fuel costs when you are driving, or to blag a ride if you don't have access to a car.

This is likely to be much cheaper and more comfortable than travelling by public transport. However, do read the safety guidance beforehand.

Rail and bus travel

In the UK, travelling by train can be an expensive business. For the budget traveller, it is always worth exploring coach fares. Travelling by road may take longer, but you are guaranteed a seat and can save a considerable amount compared to rail travel.

Megabus offers low-cost coach and bus travel between cities, as well as inexpensive fares to airports. However, GoPili will allow you to compare and find the best deal on coach fares.

If you prefer to travel by rail, booking early will often get you the most competitive price on your tickets, especially if you can do this a couple of months in advance.

Confusingly, the cost of two single rail tickets can work out cheaper than a return, so always check this before booking.

If you are eligible, it may be worth purchasing a railcard, which will give you up to a third off. These cost around £30.

Flights

Airline ticket prices vary wildly, depending on time of year, the day of the week and the time you travel. They also increase during school holidays and for events such as Christmas or other religious festivals.

If demand is high, then prices will be more expensive. Therefore, it stands to reason that if you can travel when the hoards aren't, prices will be cheaper. Flying out of season will get you the most economical air tickets. If you can be flexible about when and where you fly to, you can also save quite a lot of money.

Early morning or late-night flights will tend to offer the best value, as will flying mid-week.

Always shop around. Skyscanner, GoPili and Google Flights allow you to compare the cost of flights around the world.

Budget carriers such as Ryanair and easyJet offer amazing deals on short haul flights. It is worth downloading their apps to spot the cheapest prices.

Find free events and activities

Wherever you go on holiday, don't forget to search for free events and activities. Check tourist information websites and notice boards, and do a 'free things to do in...' type search on the Internet before you depart.

SAVE MONEY ON MOTORING

Minimising fuel consumption

If you are driving yourself for a holiday or day out, there are ways to minimise your fuel consumption.

According to the AA, you can save up to 10% on your fuel if you get your car serviced regularly to keep the engine running efficiently.

The AA also advises that you check your car manual to make sure the tyres are at the correct pressure, as under inflated tyres use more fuel. Remove roof boxes when not in use, as they add wind resistance, increasing your fuel consumption. Likewise, don't carry heavy tools around with you unless strictly necessary.

Other tips include:

Cut down on the air-con, as this increases fuel consumption. If it's a hot day, open the windows rather than turn on the air conditioning. Also turn off anything electrical in the car when you aren't using it, such as heated windscreens, fans and headlights.

If you get stuck in a traffic jam, switch off the engine. Stick to speed limits: the faster you go the more fuel you will use. You may also get a speeding ticket, which will cost you a fine and is likely to increase the cost of your insurance.

Slow down! The AA says, "Driving at 70mph uses up to 9% more fuel than at 60mph and up to 15% more than at 50mph. Cruising at 80mph can use up to 25% more fuel than at 70mph."

These small actions could add up to big savings, particularly if you use your car a lot.

Chapter 12: A Frugal Christmas

"Then the Grinch thought of something he hadn't before! What if Christmas, he thought, doesn't come from a store. What if Christmas...perhaps...means a little bit more!" — Dr. Seuss, How the Grinch Stole Christmas!

Christmas shouldn't be a surprise to you. It comes around the same time each year, after all. But, if you choose to celebrate, it can be an expensive business.

According to *Money Helper,* one in three people in the UK feel pressured to spend more than they can afford over Christmas. Fuelled by advertising, social media and family expectations, we put so much pressure on ourselves to make the festive season perfect, even if it means getting into debt.

For many of us, giving expensive gifts, having a beautifully decorated home and hosting the best Christmas meal has become a show of our own wealth and success. How is it that a tradition that is supposed to be about joy, peace and Christianity has become so fraught with stress?

You may be plagued by questions such as 'Can I buy gifts that will thrill my partner and/or children without breaking the bank? Who shall we spend time with over Christmas? Will I receive gifts I don't like?'

It's not just money that can be in short supply, but time too, as requests come in from schools to attend Christmas events, from employers for office celebrations, and invitations from friends and family to visit.

It's all in the planning

Personally, I have found Christmas seriously stressful at times. Getting ahead with planning, even if I don't intend to do anything out of the ordinary, really helps to allay the anxiety I have experienced in the past.

I have made many classic mistakes, getting a picture in my head of an impossibly perfect festive season fresh out of a glossy magazine or my Instagram feed. Like many others, I have berated myself when the house isn't decorated with the most tasteful and expensive baubles, when I couldn't afford to host the lavish parties that some of my friends did, take the kids to see Santa in Lapland, or buy every relative and friend an expensive gift.

I have bought too much food and alcohol, denting the budget and making me feel unhealthy trying to eat it all and not let it go to waste.

Christmas has gone on the credit card in past years too, meaning that it was still taking a chunk out of my monthly budget the following spring.

Not any more, though! I learned my lesson the hard way.

Our expectations of what Christmas should be are sometimes set so high, it is almost certain to be a let-down. This can leave you deflated and defeated come January, maybe dreading the credit card bills or looking sadly at your overdraft.

Of course, many people absolutely love Christmas. They have no reason to worry about any kind of post-Christmas hangovers, be they financial or alcohol induced. However, if you look forward more with a sense of dread at the potential expense and lack of time than anticipation of the fun of the occasion, this chapter is for you.

Just how can you reduce the pressure of Christmas and make it more fun without busting your bank balance or maxing out your credit cards? Can you still have an enjoyable Christmas when you are skint?

MANAGING A LOW-COST CHRISTMAS

Set a budget

The most basic way to manage Christmas when you are trying to rein in your spending is to make a budget for it and save in advance. I usually start putting away small amounts of money each month in January or February.

Write a list of all of the people you feel you need to buy for and how much you want to spend, the amount needed for food and drink, decorations, outings, etc. Calculate the total. Can you afford that much? If not, think about how you can scale down. Read on for ideas on how to do this.

I have a spreadsheet that I revise each year, as appropriate. If I can't afford the amount I calculate using the spreadsheet, I start to look for ways to reduce costs.

A cautionary tale

I often tell the story of the conversations I had with my own family about the escalating cost of Christmas. As one of four children with two surviving parents, four lots of husbands/wives and a growing number of children between us, buying for everyone had become too much for my bank balance.

I tried suggesting a token gift for the adults with a maximum budget of £5, having a second-hand challenge (buying a gift from a charity shop that might be nice or more of a joke gift) or everybody going for something handmade. There was little enthusiasm for any of these suggestions in my family, although I know others who have embraced these ideas.

Eventually, we found something we were all happy with. We agreed to buy gifts for any children up to the point where they began working. The adults were all put in a secret Santa draw with a budget of £30 each.

This meant that instead of buying for ten adults, we each only needed to buy for one. As the years have gone on and the children have grown, they have joined the secret Santa. We have gone from buying for nine children to buying for just three who are still in education (plus our own adult children, of course).

Now everybody agrees that it is a huge relief. The time, money and mental energy saved is a gift in itself.

Give yourself permission to scale down

If you are on a limited budget, give yourself permission to scale down if you need to. Think about how you might do that. Go through your list or spreadsheet and revise the amount you will spend on gifts. Are there some people you would prefer not to buy for?

For example, have you got into the habit of buying for friends and their children? Could you have a chat with your friends and explain that you can no longer afford to do this? Perhaps you could suggest you all get together for a Christmas craft session instead?

Do you need to buy gifts for your children's teachers? We rarely gave presents to school staff. Having a school secretary as a sister and several friends who are teachers, I realised just how many gifts of chocolates, toiletries and stationery they receive. A nice, homemade card or picture will probably be more appreciated.

The office Christmas party

When I worked in an office, there was a work 'do' (which we had to pay for), a team meal out, a management meal out, various drinks gatherings, a lunchtime pot luck buffet, a whole office secret Santa and a team secret Santa. I realised early on that I couldn't afford to do everything so I stuck to my team meal out and one secret Santa.

It's different if you work for a company that pays for your Christmas events – in which case, go for it! My daughter was lucky enough to go to Winter Wonderland in London one year, followed by a party on a boat on the Thames. I worked for the local council who, like me, had to spend according to their budget (which, for employee Christmas events, was precisely nothing).

It can feel awkward to say no to invitations, but in my experience, telling your work colleagues that you don't have the money to do everything, or you are focussing your spending on your children, or that you are saving for next year's holiday/new kitchen/house deposit, will be accepted at face value.

Don't apologise for living within your means and staying out of debt, at Christmas or any other time.

Christmas food – it's just one day!

The Christmas meal. Much anticipated and enjoyed, nevertheless expectations are for it to be the best dinner of the year. This puts huge pressure on the cook, and can cost a small fortune.

On top of that, many of us eat a special Christmas breakfast, tea, Christmas Eve and Boxing Day meal too! We spend too much money, and tend to buy far more than we can eat, leading to the need to eat leftovers in some form until the new year (or worse, food waste). How many of us stuff our faces until we are so full we can barely move, drink too much alcohol, and then feel guilty at piling on the pounds?

Try to remember that Christmas is just a couple of days. Plan for and buy just what you need and can afford. There is no need to purchase a big turkey unless you are cooking for a crowd (and if you are broke, try to scale that down as much as you can). Many people prefer other, cheaper meat anyway. It's just a glorified roast at the end of the day!

If no one really likes Christmas pudding, then buy what they do like. There's nothing wrong with a frozen Viennetta or apple crumble for dessert if that's what your family enjoys!

Make your own traditions

One good way to approach Christmas when you don't have much money is to make it about spending time together with the people you love instead of focussing solely on gifts. For most children, the holiday has become about waking up as early as possible to huge piles of presents. They won't remember most of these gifts. However, they probably will remember the activities you enjoyed together.

I am not suggesting expecting your children to accept activities *instead* of gifts. However, making Christmas about quality time with them rather than working as much as you can to buy them more and more stuff can be more rewarding and make them more appreciative of what they do receive.

You don't have to spend lots of money on Christmas events. Rather, you could get creative and find free or cheap activities. Make your own Christmas traditions!

Buy gifts you know people want

We have all experienced feelings of guilt and embarrassment when we have received items we don't want, and we don't want to make the same mistakes in our gift giving to others. To avoid spending your hard-earned cash purchasing presents that might not be used, listen to your family and friends to pick up hints about what they would appreciate. If you still have no clue, ask them for some ideas. Presents don't have to be a surprise. In fact, I much prefer to buy something I know the recipient will really like.

If they won't give you any hints, some good generic gift ideas for most people are food and drink, vouchers for stores, restaurants, cinemas, etc. Socks and pyjamas may seem dull, but are at least likely to be used.

Be wary of buying experiences unless you are sure they will be used before they expire. Some also involve travelling to get to them, which adds a cost to the gift, so bear that in mind.

Likewise, let people know what you like so you receive gifts you appreciate.

Don't be ashamed to buy second-hand

I frequently buy used books from charity shops as stocking fillers. It's easy enough to pick them up for 50p each or less, often in immaculate condition.

But you don't have to stop at second-hand stocking fillers. One year, when I was especially skint, I started buying my presents in the summer from boot sales. I found a remarkable number of items that were new, nearly new, or could be regarded as vintage!

A thoughtful and useful gift is just as thoughtful and useful whether you buy it new or used. If the recipient is concerned with environmental issues, they may be very pleased. I am certainly happy to receive a pre-loved item.

When you are faced with buying for children at Christmas with a limited budget, Facebook Marketplace is a great place to find second-hand toys and bikes in your local area. Most kids care about the item itself and not whether it came in a shiny new box.

FUN FRUGAL THINGS TO DO AT CHRISTMAS

There are lots of fun things to do at Christmas that won't break the bank. Here are some suggestions:

Find a Christmas carol service. Our Christmas tradition when my daughters were younger was to attend the Christmas Eve children's service at the local church. They were convinced the 'sleepy biscuits' they were given on the way out made them drift off more easily!

Visit your local town centre in the evening to see the Christmas lights. You can also take a tour of the best decorated Christmas houses in your area. We have a fantastic Christmas house a couple of streets away. For a small donation, you can even go into their front garden and get sprayed with fake snow!

Check your local council website for free events. Ours usually has the turning on of the Christmas lights, combined with a market, carol singers, dance acts and more. They also have one free event each year in early December when you can access the castle for no charge, plus a free Christmas carol concert at the local theatre. Research what is happening and book early.

Try some Christmas crafts using recycled materials and household items, such as polystyrene, cotton wool, silver foil, sweet wrappers, cardboard and fabric, supplemented with some pipe cleaners, glitter, glue and paint.

We still have some of the painted pine cones and homemade paper decorations created by my daughters years ago, including a snowman made from a cardboard toilet roll tube covered in cotton wool with pipe cleaner arms and a felt carrot nose!

Watch a Christmas movie on TV with some popcorn and a few treats.

Do some Christmas baking. It's worth investing in some Christmas biscuit cutters for this.

Make some of your own Christmas presents. Pinterest is awash with creative ideas that don't cost much.

Have a toy declutter and donate or sell good quality items. Get the children involved in this so that they learn to let things go to make space for the new.

Decorate the tree together and make some baubles.

Bake a gingerbread house. If you don't fancy starting this from scratch, you can pick up kits pretty cheaply.

Host a potluck Christmas party. Ask your guests to bring a dish and something to drink for everyone to share.

Make your own Christmas cards. You can pick up materials from the pound shop or places like Home Bargains and The Works.

Make gift tags from last year's Christmas cards. A pair of pinking shears, a hole punch and some ribbons are all handy for this.

Go for a winter walk in the woods. Get your wellies and warm clothes on and get outside. This is even better if you are lucky enough to get some snow!

Send a letter to Santa – you can find out how to do that on the Royal Mail website.

Visit a Christmas market. If you are taking children, come to an understanding in advance that you won't be making lots of purchases but will have a treat, such as a burger or a hot chocolate.

Summing up

In my experience, it is still the case that the bulk of the Christmas organisation and work is done by women. We are often trying to keep all of the traditions going, whilst holding down jobs and running a household.

Scaling down present buying and the number of events you host or attend can make the whole process more enjoyable and less stressful.

Setting a realistic budget, managing expectations and having honest conversations with your loved ones will make all the difference when you are doing Christmas on a tight budget. Making time for fun is also important, but you don't have to spend a fortune to enjoy the festive season.

Chapter 13: Health and Well-being on a Budget

"It is health that is real wealth and not pieces of gold and silver" - Mahatma Gandhi

When you are short of money, it is easy to make your own health and fitness a low priority. However, if we are blessed with good health it is our greatest gift, one that makes everything else in life possible.

As well as giving you a better quality of life, it makes financial sense to look after the physical well-being of both yourself and your family. Although we are lucky to have free health care via the NHS in the UK, it is becoming less 'free' as time goes on.

Most of us have to pay for prescriptions, for example, as well as dental treatment. There are often long waiting lists for surgical procedures and treatments such as physiotherapy.

Spending a little time on self-care can pay dividends in the long run, and make you feel so much better too. But can you do it on a budget?

FRUGAL FITNESS

We all know that exercise is important for our health. According to the NHS website, "Adults should do some type of physical activity every day. Exercise just once or twice a week can reduce the risk of heart disease or stroke."

If you can afford a gym membership (and will use it), that's great. However, you really don't need to go to the gym to get fit and lose some weight. Here are some ideas for activities that cost very little.

Exercise at home

YouTube is a brilliant place to find free exercise classes. However, bear in mind that anyone can start a YouTube channel. Do some research to find properly qualified instructors.

If you have particular health issues, I would recommend attending some classes to begin with so that you can learn about any adjustments you need to make. Speak to your doctor too.

If you have the space, you could also set a mini gym up at home. Many people buy brand new gym equipment that they swear they will use but never do, which means it is relatively easy to pick up second-hand in very good condition.

Be it a cross trainer, an exercise bike or weights, check out sites such as Gumtree and Facebook Marketplace to see what is available locally. If you are lucky, you might even be able to source unwanted items for free via Freecycle or Freegle.

You can also find inexpensive smaller items of equipment in supermarkets and discount stores like B&M or Home Bargains, particularly in the new year (and if you wait until early February, some of those items will have been heavily discounted).

Other indoor exercises or activities you could try are yoga (you just need a mat), hula hooping and stair climbing - a great way to strengthen your legs and build stamina.

Free exercise outdoors

Walking and running are free, or at least once you have paid for a decent pair of trainers or walking boots. We walk a lot and like to use an app such as Map My Walk to track how far we have travelled.

My 60-something sister started running using the Couch to 5K programme a couple of years ago, and is now running half marathons! It is a free nine-week programme that was developed by the NHS.

Once you get confident as a jogger (or even just as a walker), you can take part in a ParkRun near you. These are free community events that take place weekly all over the UK and even internationally. ParkRuns aim to be: "a positive, welcoming and inclusive experience where there is no time limit and no one finishes last." The whole family can do them, and there are even junior events.

Hands up those of you with bicycles gathering dust in the shed. Why not pump up the tyres and go for a cycle! This is nice for all the family to do together on a sunny day and very good for building fitness.

It is also worth looking for outdoor gyms and fitness trails in public parks. Check your local council website to find some near you.

Staying fit doesn't need to cost a fortune and you definitely don't need a personal trainer.

Group activities

There are usually group activities to enjoy that can be inexpensive. Many council leisure centres offer sports like football, netball, basketball, badminton, tennis and swimming at reasonable prices.

Alternatively, gather family and friends together to play ball games at the park.

Free passes

Many gyms and fitness centres offer free trials and day passes. Even if you have no intention of joining, you can still go from time to time as a freebie.

Check local newspapers, websites and the leaflets that come through your door for free passes.

However, do be aware that the gym staff will try to sign you up as a member, so be prepared and remember there is no obligation.

A HOLISTIC APPROACH TO HEALTH

There are other simple frugal steps you can take to improve your health. Here are some ideas that will cost very little:

Drink plenty of water

Do you drink enough water? Keeping hydrated is important for the health of your heart, kidneys and liver. It also improves your exercise performance and helps prevent headaches.

Nothing is cheaper or easier to improve your health and appearance than drinking water. Wrinkles show more on dehydrated skin and drinking lots of water flushes out toxins and improves blood flow, so your skin will look better.

Eat a healthy diet

Assess your diet too and see where it could be improved. There is plenty of evidence to suggest that foods high in sugar and fat are bad for us and that most people do not eat enough fruit and vegetables.

Cutting out the snacks and takeaways will actually save you money. If you are overweight, look at your portion sizes too. By cooking from scratch a lot of the time, not only will you spend less on food; you will also likely eat less sugar, fat and salt, and consume fewer preservatives.

Finally, make sure you get your five portions of fruit and vegetables every day.

Sleep well

Try to get enough sleep. This will help you physically and mentally. Lack of sleep can lead to mindless snacking if you are low on energy.

I am the worst for not going to bed when I need to, yet I look and feel so much better if I get my 7-8 hours a night. Sleep experts will tell you to turn off all of your screens a good half hour before bed.

Deal with stress

Stress is unavoidable, but dealing with it is essential. Constant stress over a long period can have detrimental effects on your health. According to the Stress Management Society, long term stress "is now known to contribute to heart disease, hypertension and high blood pressure, it affects the immune system, is linked to strokes, IBS, ulcers, diabetes, muscle and joint pain, miscarriage, allergies, alopecia and even premature tooth loss."

As a trained yoga teacher, I understand the benefits of a regular yoga practice on reducing stress. At £10 a class in some places, though, it may be out of your budget to attend every week.

There are some excellent online resources. As a starting point, check out Yoga with Adriene on YouTube.

Meditation is also well known for helping to reduce stress levels and improve mood. There are some free apps that can get you started on this. Calm and Headspace both offer some basic practices for nothing.

Keep it simple. Sometimes just sitting quietly and counting each breath from one to 10 for five minutes can be effective for quieting your mind.

Other good ways to lower stress that don't cost much include taking up pretty much any form of exercise, going for a walk in nature, having a hot bubble bath, doing a craft, or simply indulging in any activity that you enjoy. Allow time to unwind now and again.

BEAUTY ON A BUDGET

You can spend a fortune on looking good, but I know many women who manage to be gorgeous without breaking the bank. Just because you are frugal it doesn't mean you have to be frumpy. Taking care of yourself makes you feel better mentally as well as physically, but you don't need a huge budget. There are lots of things you can do to save money. Here are some ideas.

Trade down

As with food, there are often amazing bargains on toiletries and beauty products in discount supermarkets such as Aldi and Lidl.

For example, you can spend £50 plus on a wrinkle busting moisturiser. However, when you are on a tight budget it has got to be worth trying Aldi's £3 pot, hasn't it?

Personally, I gave up on all the marketing hype around beauty products a long time ago. I need to use a moisturiser, but have happily traded down and never spend more than around £5.

I take the same approach to most other makeup and beauty products and have saved hundreds of pounds over the years as a result.

Dilute your shampoo - or give it up!

Most of us use more shampoo than we need. But it is possible to use a bit less by really soaking your hair and then using shampoo diluted with water.

Some people stop washing their hair altogether. This 'no poo' concept has many devotees, who say giving up shampoo and all hair products leaves their hair looking better than it ever did when they piled on the chemicals. You can simply rinse your hair with water, although some people use cider vinegar as a rinse or rub baking soda into their scalp before rinsing.

Cut your own hair

In the past I have saved money by cutting my own hair, as well as my daughter's. I was never brave enough to do a restyle; I just trimmed the ends. My daughter has very long straight hair, so I followed a YouTube tutorial that involved tying it into a high ponytail and snipping off a few inches. It worked really well, giving her a few long layers.

Find a hairdressing student

If you are not brave (or foolhardy) enough to cut your own hair, you could put yourself in the hands of a hairdressing student. This could be at a hair and beauty college or in a salon. Our local college charges £7.50 for a cut and blow dry at the time of writing, although I have had a completely free cut done by a trainee at a hairdressing salon.

I have never had a bad experience having my hair cut by a student. However, the downside is that students need their tutors to check their work regularly, so it takes twice as long as a qualified stylist.

Cheaper beauty treatments

As with haircuts, the best way to get cheap beauty treatments is to find a trainee willing to practice on you. You can get everything way cheaper, from a massage to eyebrow waxing. I recommend checking out your local further education college.

At our hair and beauty college, a luxury manicure or pedicure will set you back £10, a bikini wax is £5 and a 'slim and firm' body treatment is £12.

Give yourself a hot oil treatment

Very dry hair can benefit from a DIY hot oil treatment. Coconut oil is good, as is olive oil, but almost any oil will be beneficial. Just warm it gently, smooth it through your dry hair and wrap it in a warm towel. Leave on for 45 minutes to an hour, then shampoo off thoroughly.

Face masks

You can buy face masks fairly cheaply from places like Poundland, Home Bargains and Superdrug. However, it is even more cost effective to make your own. My daughter likes this one, which is said to help clear spots and acne:

1 teaspoon each of oatmeal, runny honey and plain yoghurt.

Just mix together and smooth over your face, avoiding the eyes. Leave on for 10-15 minutes then rinse off and use your usual moisturiser.

Boost your eyelashes

Another beauty on a budget tip that my daughter swears by is castor oil for making her eyelashes grow. She dips an old mascara or eyeliner brush into a £2 bottle of the stuff and uses it most nights.

Castor oil moisturises your lashes, thus strengthening them and enabling them to grow longer.

Use your gifts

How many times have you been given boxed sets of smellies only to stick them in the back of the cupboard and forget about them? Get them out and use them up. If you really don't like them, then re-gift them and buy yourself something you do like with the money you save.

I always drop big hints as Christmas approaches for lovely body butters and other fancy products that I wouldn't usually buy myself.

Making your hair dryer last

A common scenario: you are blowing drying your hair for a night out when your dryer begins to emit an acrid burning smell, signalling its upcoming demise. In the past I have gone through a hairdryer in under 12 months, whereas now I make them last for years.

The trick is to make sure you buy one with at least a two year guarantee and never use it on full power, as this is what makes them blow. My current one is four years old but I hope it will keep going for a while yet. I blow dry my hair every couple of days so I work it quite hard.

Use things up

I make other things last too. As well as shampoo, I have been known to water down shower gel and conditioner, I squeeze the last drop of toothpaste out of the tube by snipping the top off and the same with foundation. I found that putting a little baby oil on the mascara wand as it neared the end made it last longer too, but not too much or it ends up sliding down your face!

Cheaper glasses

Annoyingly, my once perfect vision has gone downhill in the last 20 years, meaning frequent changes of spectacles. Glasses can cost a pretty penny, especially if you have a complicated prescription.

One way to save money on specs is to ask your optician for your prescription, take it away and buy them online. I found some companies claiming to offer frames from just £6, with many designer styles at half the cost of a high street optician.

Although you can upload your photo and do a virtual try on, the downside is that you won't know exactly what they look like until you receive them. You also won't get the tweaks to the fit that you get in the shop. However, you will save money.

Chapter 14: It *Is* Easy Being Green

"...repurposing would-be throw away stuff isn't just about saving you money. It's also about helping to save the planet."
- Jeff Yeager, from his book Don't Throw That Away!

I have long realised that frugality and sustainability are natural bedfellows. It is logical that if you consume less and waste less you can help the environment as well as your bank balance.

Sure, my initial reasoning behind embracing a frugal lifestyle was to save money. I was on a suddenly reduced income and needed to get through to the end of each month. However, being frugal also appealed to the eco-warrior in me.

Swimming against the tide of consumerism

If we buy fewer things, we spend less, obviously. But when we swim against the tide of consumerism and stop buying mindlessly, the returns don't just mean we free up money to save, pay debts or simply live better. Becoming conscious about each purchase also enables us to help the environment.

We become creative with what we have, meaning that something new doesn't need to be produced, packaged and transported. In addition, by using what we already own, we don't clutter our homes with more unwanted items.

For example, how often do we impulse buy clothes when we already have a wardrobe full of things we hardly wear? Clothing we bought on a whim, only to find we have five T-shirts the same or that the new purchase doesn't go with anything else, doesn't suit us or actually even fit?

It's not just clothing, of course. Some of us redecorate and refurbish our homes every few years when it's not essential. We upgrade our phones and other technology because we don't want to be left behind. We buy endless unnecessary 'stuff' on a whim, caving into clever marketing and perceived social pressures.

Questions to ask as a conscious consumer

It's worth stopping to think before mindlessly buying. Learn to become a conscious consumer.

Ask yourself: do I really need this? Can I afford it? If you can, ask yourself if it is worth the money? Could you get it cheaper or maybe second-hand? Maybe you will decide you don't need it after all.

Go one step further to help the environment and ask: How far did this have to travel to get here? Could I buy more locally? Is it over-packaged? What is it made from? Is there a more planet-friendly version available?

Being more mindful in the choices you make when spending your hard-earned cash can help you to shop sustainably to help the environment and allow you stick to your budget.

Let's bring together some of the money-saving ideas I have presented so far that are also more sustainable.

GOING GREEN AND SAVING MONEY

Buy second-hand to help the environment

If we buy second-hand, not only does it save us money but it potentially stops an item going to landfill.

Buying second-hand also means that the item isn't being produced from scratch, saving on the energy involved in its production and transportation, not to mention the packaging.

Buy reusable items

Nappies, handkerchiefs, sanitary products, cotton wool, dishcloths, kitchen towels and so on all have reusable options. They cost a little more to begin with, but save money over time and prevent a lot of waste. Forget using disposable wipes for cleaning. Get yourself a mop and make washable cleaning cloths from old T-shirts or towels.

Frugal food

Being thrifty in the kitchen is good for your wallet obviously, but a frugal approach to food also cuts down on food waste. The less we waste, the less we have to buy. Food waste costs us an average of around £800 per year per family, but also rotting food in landfill creates methane, a greenhouse gas.

Plan your meals and shop with a list. Freeze leftovers for a quick ready meal. Make stock from chicken carcasses and vegetable peelings and then make soup. This is really good for using up veg that is on the turn or leftovers, especially mashed potato.

Cleaning products

As I said in my chapter on frugal cleaning, the marketers will tell us that we need a different product for every job – even each room of the house. They also fill our homes with a chemical cocktail of nasties that can be bad for our health and the environment.

I prefer a simpler approach and use old fashioned products such as soda crystals, white vinegar and citric acid. It saves you money if you make some of your own cleaning products, reduces plastic packaging and, as a bonus, there will be fewer chemicals in your home. This is obviously better for the environment as well as your health.

Days out

When you go out for the day with the family, pack a picnic and take water and coffee in reusable containers. This saves money and side steps all the packaging that comes with take away food.

I keep two lightweight reusable coffee cups in my handbag and my water bottle comes everywhere with me. Even if I am just out and about, I usually have an apple or cereal bar about my person to prevent sudden hunger pangs tempting me into McDonald's...

Growing your own

Organic food means fewer chemicals, but you usually have to pay a premium. However, if you have a bit of garden, you could start to grow a few vegetables. Packets of seeds are so cheap and produce loads of plants.

Homegrown produce uses less water and fewer chemicals, needs no transportation and entails no packaging.

You can compost your raw kitchen scraps too to use in the garden to keep the soil healthy. It's cheap and saves them from landfill.

Cycling or walking

For short trips, we can save ourselves a lot of money on fuel if we use our legs to walk or cycle rather than jumping in the car without thinking. It's a cheap way to get fit too, so you could ditch the gym membership.

Saving energy

As I work from home, I have found a few tricks to keep our energy bills as low as possible and help the environment in the process.

I religiously turn off the lights when I leave a room. When I am sitting for long periods at my laptop, I can start to feel the chill. However, by layering up and keeping a blanket nearby I can avoid putting the heating on. I also move around the house with the sun. It gets very warm in the sitting room in the morning, but is better in the bedroom in the afternoon!

We have a wood burner in the lounge as well, which means it is easy to heat just that room rather than switching on the gas heating for the entire house.

Small changes such as the above really can have an impact on how much you spend as well as helping the environment. For me, these actions make me feel in control and positive, rather than deprived in any way.

Thanks for taking the time to read this book. I hope you have been inspired to embrace a frugal lifestyle and take some tips from your grandparents and great-grandparents.

I don't want to take you back to the stone age. However, there is no doubt that readopting some of the habits of our recent ancestors will save money and allow us to live more simple and sustainable lives.

Hopefully, you have learned new ways to set your finances on track, reach your financial goals and help you to pay off debts.

Don't forget to check out my YouTube channel (Shoestring Jane) and my blog Shoestring Cottage (www.shoestringcottage.com) for lots more advice and tips on living a great life on a budget.

References

I have mentioned Dave Ramsey several times throughout this book. He has much helpful advice in his various publications and on his website, https://www.ramseysolutions.com/

Chapter 1: Frugal Foundations

Citizens Advice Bureau for free advice on life: https://www.citizensadvice.org.uk/

Step Change for free advice on debt: https://www.stepchange.org/

Pay Plan - free solutions for people with multiple debts: https://www.payplan.com/

National Debtline - free and independent debt advice over the phone and online.

Debt Advice Foundation - free, confidential debt advice: https://www.debtadvicefoundation.org/

Chapter 2: Stuff, stuff and more stuff (plus how to buy less of it)

The Buyerarchy of Needs was created by Sarah Lazarovic: https://www.sarahl.com/

Freegle: https://www.ilovefreegle.org/

Freecycle: https://www.freecycle.org/

Chapter 3: Cooking and Eating Like Grandma

Waste and Resources Action Programme (WRAP): https://wrap.org.uk/

Scott Nash, the blogger who ate only expired food for a year: https://scottscompostpile.com/

Veganism is 'single biggest way' to reduce our environmental impact on planet, study finds - The Independent (https://www.independent.co.uk/life-style/health-and-families/veganism-environmental-impact-planet-reduced-plant-based-diet-humans-study-a8378631.html)

Meat Free Mondays site: https://meatfreemondays.com/

Vegetarian Society: https://vegsoc.org/

How I Lived a Year on Just a Pound a Day by Kath Kelly, ISBN 978-1-906593-12-4

Jordon Cox, aka the Coupon Kid: https://jordoncox.com/

John the Poacher on Instagram: https://www.instagram.com/johnthepoacher/

Food For Free by Richard Mabey, ISBN 978-0007183036

Olio, an app to help share waste food: https://olioex.com/

Too Good To Go, an app to help businesses to sell excess food: https://toogoodtogo.co.uk/en-gb/

Chapter 4: Granny's advice - 'Make do & Mend' and 'Waste Not, Want Not'

My Second Hand & Frugal Life Facebook group: https://www.facebook.com/groups/1015664032263189

Which? article on keeping your tumble dryer working efficiently: https://www.which.co.uk/news/2020/07/six-simple-tips-to-maintain-your-tumble-dryer/

Frenchic Fan Forum Facebook group: https://www.facebook.com/groups/411202492387852

Chapter 5: Buying Second-Hand and Getting Everything for Less

Buying second-hand:

https://www.gumtree.com/

https://www.shpock.com/en-gb

https://www.preloved.co.uk/eBay

https://onlineshop.oxfam.org.uk/

https://www.depop.com/

https://www.vinted.co.uk/

https://www.secondhand.org.uk/

https://www.facebook.com/marketplace/

https://trashnothing.com/

The Moneyless Man, Mark Boyle, ISBN 978-1-85268-754-1, https://oneworld-publications.com/

Competition sites:

https://superlucky.me/

https://www.loquax.co.uk/

http://theprizehub.co.uk/

Competition thread at Money Saving Expert: https://forums.moneysavingexpert.com/categories/competitions-time

Cashback sites:

https://www.topcashback.co.uk/

https://www.quidco.com/

Chapter 6: Slashing Your Monthly Bills

Which? article on the cost of LED bulbs: https://www.which.co.uk/reviews/light-bulbs/article/how-to-buy-the-best-light-bulb-a5ZLF4v6VDlw

https://energysavingtrust.org.uk/

https://lookaftermybills.com/

MSE site for council tax banding check: https://www.moneysavingexpert.com/reclaim/council-tax-bands-change/#overpaying

Chapter 7: Making a Frugal Home

Downsizing: http://www.tinyhouseuk.co.uk/

Property Guardianship: https://dotdotdotproperty.com

Rent a Room Scheme: https://www.gov.uk/rent-room-in-your-home/the-rent-a-room-scheme

https://www.spareroom.com/

Organisations looking for host families:

https://www.sejour-linguistique-lec.fr/

https://www.homestay.com/

https://www.ef.co.uk/host-family/hosting-foreign-students/

https://www.kaplaninternational.com/learn-english-united-kingdom/london

Become an airbnb host: https://www.airbnb.co.uk/host/homes?

https://www.theatredigsbooker.com/

The Lady Magazine jobs section: https://jobs.lady.co.uk/

Second-hand furniture shops:

https://emmaus.org.uk/

https://www.bhf.org.uk/shop

Free paint to prevent waste: https://communityrepaint.org.uk/

How to reuse wool:
http://knittingonthenet.com/learn/reuse.htm

Chapter 8: The Frugal Cleaner

The Guardian's Eco Guide to Wet Wipes:
https://www.theguardian.com/environment/2016/nov/20/the-eco-guide-to-wet-wipes

Natural Household Cleaning by Rachelle Strauss, ISBN 978-1-5048-0031-0, IMM Lifestyle Books.

Guardian article: *Explained: the toxic threat in everyday products, from toys to plastic*:
https://www.theguardian.com/us-news/2019/may/22/toxic-chemicals-everyday-items-us-pesticides-bpa

Eco Watch article, *Why you need to ditch dryer sheets*:
https://www.ecowatch.com/why-you-need-to-ditch-dryer-sheets-1881714654.html

Today article: *10 things your plumber wishes you wouldn't do*: https://www.today.com/home/10-things-your-plumber-wishes-you-wouldn-t-do-t78011

Which? article on ironing water:
https://www.which.co.uk/reviews/steam-irons/article/how-to-iron-your-clothes-a9FIY2X53qCF#should-you-use-ironing-water

Chapter 9: The Frugal Garden

Life After Money Ilona's summerhouse on a budget:
http://meanqueen-lifeaftermoney.blogspot.com/p/blog-page_8.html

Chapter 10: Frugal fashion: dress for Less

For second-hand clothing:

https://www.ebay.co.uk/

https://www.vinted.co.uk/

https://www.depop.com/

The Penny Pinchers Book, by John and Irma Mustoe, ISBN 0-285-63285-X

Cheap new clothing: https://www.everything5pounds.com/

Chapter 11: Frugal Fun and Travel

Real Junk Food Project: https://www.trjfpcentral.co.uk/

Hiking app: https://www.alltrails.com/

Open gardens info:

https://www.opengardens.co.uk/

https://ngs.org.uk/

Activities run by Age UK:
https://www.ageuk.org.uk/services/in-your-area/social-activities/

Activities run by U3a: https://www.u3a.org.uk/events

Find places to go:

https://www.wildlifetrusts.org/

https://www.visitbritain.com/gb/

https://freshwaterhabitats.org.uk/

Geocaching info: https://www.ordnancesurvey.co.uk/

Holidays and travel:

The Sun holidays: https://www.thesun.co.uk/travel/13208886/how-book-9-50-holidays/

Working farm holidays: https://wwoof.org.uk/

YHA: https://www.yha.org.uk/

https://www.airbnb.co.uk/

https://www.couchsurfing.com/

https://www.blablacar.co.uk/

https://liftshare.com/uk

https://uk.megabus.com/

https://www.gopili.co.uk/

Chapter 12: Christmas

https://www.moneyhelper.org.uk/en

Write to Santa: https://www.postoffice.co.uk/default/write-to-santa

Chapter 13

https://www.mapmywalk.com/

Couch to 5K: https://www.nhs.uk/live-well/exercise/running-and-aerobic-exercises/get-running-with-couch-to-5k/

https://www.parkrun.org.uk/

Stress Management Society: https://www.stress.org.uk/

Yoga with Adriene: https://www.youtube.com/channel/UCFKE7WVJfvaHW5q283SxchA

https://www.calm.com/

Acknowledgements

I would like to thank the following wonderful people for their help and encouragement:

My parents, Shirley and Ron, who thoughtfully passed me the frugal genes.

To my long-suffering partner in frugality, Justin, who occasionally rolls his eyes at my money saving experiments, but puts up with me anyway.

To my beautiful daughters, Beccy, Chloe and Izzy, who have inherited a passion for a bargain and who helped to proofread this book.

To all of my blog readers, YouTube subscribers and members of My Second Hand & Frugal Life community, for their constant inspiration and encouraging comments.

Back cover portrait photograph by Alistair Veryard: https://alistairveryard.com. Used courtesy of Andy Webb at UK Money Bloggers, https://ukmoneybloggers.com.

Connect with the Author

Want to stay in touch with Jane and be the first to hear about her new books?

Social media links:

Instagram: @shoestringcottage

Twitter: @shoestringjane

YouTube: Shoestring Jane

Facebook: My Second Hand & Frugal Life

Website: www.shoestringcottage.com

If you enjoyed this book, don't forget to leave a review on Amazon! I highly appreciate your reviews, and it only takes a minute to do.

Printed in Great Britain
by Amazon